The Case for the Centre Right

The Case for the Centre Right

Edited by
DAVID GAUKE

polity

First published in 2023 by Polity Press

Polity Press
65 Bridge Street
Cambridge CB2 1UR, UK

Polity Press
111 River Street
Hoboken, NJ 07030, USA

ISBN-13: 978-1-5095-6081-3 (hardback)
ISBN-13: 978-1-5095-6082-0 (paperback)

A catalogue record for this book is available from the British Library.

Library of Congress Control Number: 2023938220

Typeset in 11 on 13 pt Warnock Pro
by Cheshire Typesetting Ltd, Cuddington, Cheshire
Printed and bound in Great Britain by CPI Group (UK) Ltd, Croydon

For further information on Polity, visit our website:
politybooks.com

Contents

About the Authors

David Gauke is a former Conservative MP and cabinet minister, serving as Chief Secretary to the Treasury, Work and Pensions Secretary, Justice Secretary and Lord Chancellor. He lost the Conservative whip for opposing a no deal Brexit and fought the 2019 general election as an Independent. He is now a regular columnist for the *New Statesman* and *ConservativeHome*.

Andrew Cooper served as Director of Strategy to Prime Minister David Cameron during the Conservative–Liberal Democrat coalition government. He is founder of the polling consultancy Populus and advises businesses and campaigns on strategy. He was appointed to the House of Lords in 2014 as Lord Cooper of Windrush. He is also a visiting lecturer at the London School of Economics.

Rory Stewart is President of GiveDirectly and the co-presenter with Alastair Campbell of *The Rest Is Politics*. He was an MP from 2010–19, serving as a minister in DEFRA, DfiD, FCO and MoJ and finally as Development Secretary. Before entering politics, he served as a British diplomat, ran a charity in

Afghanistan and had a chair at Harvard University. His books include the *New York Times* bestseller *The Places in Between*, which records his 21-month walk across Asia.

Dominic Grieve is a barrister and King's Counsel and a visiting Professor at Goldsmiths, University of London. He was MP for Beaconsfield from 1997 to 2019, sitting as a Conservative before becoming an Independent, as a result of having the whip withdrawn over his opposition to a no-deal Brexit. He was Attorney General for England and Wales from 2010–14, served in the government of David Cameron and was Chair of the Intelligence and Security Committee of Parliament from 2015–19.

Gavin Barwell had a long career in Conservative politics, serving as the party's Director of Campaigning, the MP for Croydon Central from 2010 to 2017, a government minister and Downing Street Chief of Staff for the last two years of Theresa May's premiership. He has written about the latter experience in *Chief of Staff: Notes from Downing Street*. He is the co-founder of NorthStar, which advises global businesses on geopolitical risk.

Tim Pitt served as a special adviser at the Treasury to Chancellors Philip Hammond and Sajid Javid. Since leaving the Treasury in 2019, Tim has been a partner at the business consultancy Flint Global and written widely on economic and fiscal policy, including for the *Telegraph* and the *Financial Times*. He is also a Policy Fellow at the think tank Onward. Prior to going into politics, Tim was a corporate lawyer at the City firm Slaughter and May.

Anne Milton is a former nurse who worked in the NHS for 25 years before being elected as a Conservative MP. She was a Minister for Public Health, Minister for Skills and

Apprenticeships and Government Deputy Chief Whip. She now chairs a Social Value Recruitment Board for PeoplePlus; is an associate for KPMG; Chairs the Purpose Health Coalition; and is an advisor to PLMR. She continues to work for a number of organisations on skills and further education.

Sam Gyimah served as a government minister with responsibility for higher education, science, research and innovation, and was Parliamentary Private Secretary to David Cameron. Elected to parliament in 2010, he was the Conservative MP for East Surrey from 2010–19 and, for a brief period at the end of 2019, he was a Liberal Democrat MP. Sam started his career as an investment banker and continues to advise a number of venture capital and private equity firms with a focus on geopolitics and financing the innovation economy. He is also a non-executive director of Goldman Sachs International.

Amber Rudd is a former politician who held cabinet roles under David Cameron, Theresa May and Boris Johnson. As Secretary of State for Energy and Climate Change, she led the UK delegation at the Paris Climate agreement in 2015. She left parliament at the end of 2019 and pursues a career in the energy transition working in the private sector and on policy initiatives to influence government policy.

Michael Heseltine was a member of parliament from 1966 to 2001. During this time he held various cabinet positions, including First Secretary of State and Deputy Prime Minister under John Major. He has continued to work and publish on issues of growth, industrial strategy and devolution. A fierce campaigner for Remain, he became President of The European Movement in 2019. He is also founder and Chairman of the Haymarket Group, a privately owned media company.

Daniel Finkelstein OBE is a columnist for *The Times* and the author of *Everything in Moderation* and a family memoir, *Hitler, Stalin, Mum and Dad*. He provided political advice to Prime Ministers John Major, David Cameron and Theresa May, and was director of policy for William Hague during his time as opposition leader. In 2013 he was appointed to the House of Lords.

Introduction

David Gauke

If one had asked an informed international observer to describe the nature of politics and political opinion in the United Kingdom, until relatively recently the answer would most likely have been along the following lines . . .

The United Kingdom does not have a doctrinaire antipathy to big government in the way that, for example, might be attributed to the United States, but it is more sceptical than many other European nations. It broadly tends to favour market solutions wherever possible. It is generally cautious when it comes to government borrowing and debt but, if affordable, is keen to maintain competitiveness on matters of taxation.

This stems, in part, from its belief in economic openness. It sees itself as a trading nation, favours lowering barriers to trade, and seeks to attract foreign investment and talent to its shores. Its economy is relatively focused on sectors that are international in character, such as financial services, the creative arts and technology, and this contributes to an outward-looking approach.

It is more generally internationalist in nature, playing a wholehearted role in the defence of its values and allies. It is an enthusiastic member of the North Atlantic Treaty

Organisation (NATO). As for the European Union, it is clearly sceptical about a federalist vision of a United States of Europe but it has also played a vital and constructive role in the creation of the European Single Market and in enlarging the EU to encompass the nations of eastern and central Europe.

The UK is a nation of strong institutions: parliament, an impartial civil service and an independent judiciary. The rule of law is venerated. The 1970s was certainly a turbulent decade but British politics is largely stable and produces leaders who – while not necessarily perfect – are conscientious, public-spirited, and sensible.

In general, the UK would be described as pragmatic, sceptical of the ideology of left or right, willing to embrace the future but appreciative of the value of continuity. British governments reflected the electorate and, crucially, general elections were usually won by the party that made the most compelling pitch to the centre ground of British politics. More often than not, that party would be the Conservative Party.

Our observer might go on to state that the nature of British politics and the nature of the Conservative Party were closely aligned. For the most part, the Conservatives represented the cautious and pragmatic instincts of the British public. Even when led from the right – as happened during Margaret Thatcher's time in office – Conservative governments sought to deliver a pro-business environment, a stable and certain political environment, and a constructive relationship with our neighbours. Ministers would be appointed on the basis of their political and administrative abilities, rather than on ideological purity.

The one recent extended period when the Conservative Party was unsuccessful in winning elections was when the party was perceived as no longer representing these values. In the 1997, 2001 and 2005 general elections, the Conservatives were seen, initially, as divided, exhausted and out-of-touch but then, increasingly, as extreme and ideological. Electoral matters were not helped by the fact that the Labour Party was led by Tony Blair, who was viewed by much of the electorate as sharing many of the instincts of moderate Conservatives. The Tories only returned to office after (a) Blair had gone and (b) the Conservatives had engaged on a conscious programme of modernisation that sought to reposition them in the centre ground of British politics.

Even then, the Conservatives failed to obtain an outright majority in 2010 and governed in coalition with the Liberal Democrats. To the surprise of both parties, the Coalition government proved to be remarkably stable and considerable common ground was found between the David Cameron-led Conservatives and the Nick Clegg-led Liberal Democrats.

It did the Liberal Democrats little good. In the 2015 general election their centre left voters abandoned them to support Labour while their centre right voters decided that they might as well vote Tory. With Labour having moved to the left under Ed Miliband, the Conservatives won a parliamentary majority for the first time in twenty-three years. With Labour shortly afterwards moving much further to the left – under Jeremy Corbyn – our observer would most probably have concluded that the Conservatives would be the dominant force of British politics for years to come; and that the liberal centre right would continue to be the pre-eminent force in British politics. Our observer would have been half right. The Conservatives remained in office, albeit losing their majority in 2017, before obtaining a landslide victory in 2019. The values and policies of the liberal centre right – the dominant form of British politics from 1979 onwards – was, however, in decline. British politics was changing. The electorate was already slowly rea-ligning but this process accelerated in 2016 with the Brexit referendum. Under Boris Johnson, the Conservatives leant into this realignment, appealing to voters of a more authoritar-ian and nationalistic instinct. The choice paid rich dividends for Johnson, delivering an 80-seat majority, the largest

Conservative majority since 1987. The Conservatives were dominant but, as this book argues, by and large, the liberal centre right had been marginalised.

The politics of the Conservative Party became more populist under Johnson, followed (briefly) by a period of ill-considered ideological purity under Liz Truss. This left our economy weaker, our standing in the world diminished, our political standards cheapened and our institutions destabilised. Rishi Sunak has repaired some of the damage but leads a party that has not yet fully returned to its mainstream traditions.

The purpose of this book is to argue that the marginalisation of the liberal centre right is detrimental to the country and urgently needs to be reversed.

How Brexit changed everything . . . and the forces that led to it

The 2016 EU referendum was a pivotal moment in British politics, bringing an end to David Cameron's premiership and beginning a period of great political volatility. It was a disastrous moment for the liberal centre right. The decision to call a referendum and the result, however, did not come from nowhere. It was the culmination of decades of growing Euroscepticism inside and outside the Conservative Party.

At the time of the first European referendum in 1975, it was the Labour Party that was split and the Conservatives who were overwhelmingly united in support of membership of what was then the European Economic Community. A small minority of Conservative MPs, led by Enoch Powell, had opposed the UK joining in the parliamentary debate of 1972; by 1975 Powell had left the party. The new Tory leader, Margaret Thatcher, had no hesitation in supporting the campaign to stay.

Labour, meanwhile, was more deeply divided. The Labour left – including cabinet ministers such as Tony Benn, Barbara

Castle and Peter Shore – campaigned to Leave, while those on the Labour right – such as Roy Jenkins – enthusiastically backed Remain. The Prime Minister, Harold Wilson, recommended remaining but maintained a low profile during the campaign.

With most mainstream politicians, plus most of the newspapers, business and the trades unions favouring a vote to stay in, the British public voted 2–1 in favour of Europe.

By 1983, with people like Jenkins having left Labour to form the Social Democratic Party, Labour had moved to favouring leaving the European Economic Community. The Conservatives, however, remained steadfastly in favour of membership, even if Mrs Thatcher's relationship with European institutions was not entirely cordial. She won the general election by a landslide. The matter appeared largely settled.

It was during the following parliament that a former Conservative Minister, Arthur Cockburn, as European Commissioner, put in place the European Single Market, which involved member states surrendering their vetoes in order to remove non-tariff barriers. Internal opposition to the move within the Conservative Party was limited to the fringes, and the relevant legislation sailed serenely through parliament.

For the vast majority of Thatcher's premiership, the UK's relationship with Europe was not a first-order issue. She was never an enthusiast for close integration within Europe but saw efforts to reduce trade barriers within the European Community as consistent with her beliefs in free trade and free markets.

The mood began to change in the late 1980s, with the pivotal month being September 1988. First, the President of the European Commission delivered a speech to the TUC conference in Bournemouth on 8 September, in which he argued that Europe enabled workers' rights to be protected. He was well received, indicating that the left was moving away from its

Euroscepticism. Second, on 20 September, Margaret Thatcher responded by delivering the Bruges Speech, the founding text of Conservative Euroscepticism.

Read today, the Bruges Speech appears remarkably moderate in that Thatcher declares that 'our destiny is in Europe, as part of the Community'. But she argues against a federal Europe and raises concerns that Europe is moving in the direction of higher levels of regulation. 'We have not successfully rolled back the frontiers of the state in Britain, only to see them re-imposed at a European level with a European super-state exercising a new dominance from Brussels', Thatcher declared.

Euroscepticism was now made up of two elements. The first was the longstanding argument about sovereignty. The second was an argument coming from the free market right – that Europe had an agenda that was economically interventionist and anti-markets. To put it another way, Europe was anti-Thatcherite.

It was in this context that a growing number of Thatcher's strongest supporters became increasingly Eurosceptic. The ignominious nature of sterling's departure from the Exchange Rate Mechanism – membership of which was a policy advocated by mainstream opinion – only strengthened the confidence of those who questioned the pro-European consensus.

By the mid-1990s, Euroscepticism was a strong force in the Conservative Party, making the life of the Prime Minister increasingly difficult. Thatcherites felt aggrieved at the loss of their political heroine and much of the debate had by this point focused on membership of the Euro, with the bulk of the Conservative Party opposing the UK's participation. It was one of the few issues on which the Tories were more obviously in line with public opinion than their opponents, even if the public did not see it as a priority issue.

Tory Euroscepticism was strong but it generally still favoured continued membership of the EU. 'In Europe, not run by Europe', was William Hague's slogan, having become party leader following the landslide defeat in 1997. Most Conservatives took the Eurosceptic side of the debate but the debate was not about whether we left the EU but whether we should become more closely integrated into it. For many Eurosceptic Conservatives, thus far but no further was a perfectly satisfactory position.

This remained the default position for many Conservatives, almost until the referendum campaign of 2016. Few Conservative MPs made the case that we would be 'better off out' during the coalition years, but distanced themselves from the frontbench by advocating a referendum on EU membership. Such a position went down well with those party members who were unhappy with the inevitable concessions that have to be made in a coalition and who disliked socially liberal policies such as gay marriage. It was also a means of neutralising the threat of the UK Independence Party, led by Nigel Farage, who had become an electoral force in European parliamentary elections.

The demand for a referendum grew stronger. Cameron – mindful of holding the Conservative Party together and believing that resolving the issue in favour of remaining was most likely to happen if the matter was addressed sooner rather than later – announced that a Conservative government would hold an in–out referendum.

This is not a detailed account of the Brexit referendum; however, there are certain points that flow from that period that are important in understanding the current state of the centre right in British politics.

The first, as I have mentioned, is that relatively few Conservative MPs were committed to leaving the EU in advance of the campaign. For some, this was tactical. Steve Baker, for example, was always going to favour leaving the EU but did not announce his position until negotiations were complete, at which point he declared his disappointment at the outcome. Given his absolutist position on sovereignty, he

must have known that there was no prospect of the renego-
tiations satisfying his conditions. For others, who may have
identified as Eurosceptics, leaving had not been their biggest
priority. But now that the question of membership was in
front of them, they gave the Eurosceptic answer, even if it
was a very different question from the one that was asked in
previous years.

The second, as became apparent in subsequent years, was
the widespread naivety about what leaving would mean. Many
Leave-supporting Conservative MPs genuinely believed that
we would get much the same access to European markets as
we had as EU members, even if we no longer had to follow the
rules of the Single Market. The German car manufacturers
would see to it. As for Northern Ireland, the problems with
the border were dismissed. It was not even worth trying to
understand the issue.

Some will say this is too generous an explanation. They must
have known that we would lose access to EU markets, it was
obvious to anyone who understood the issue. Some Leavers,
of course, did understand and thought it a price worth paying.
But not all. Boris Johnson, for example, according to Dominic
Cummings, by autumn 2020 still did not understand the difference between the Single Market and the Customs Union,
even though he had led the Leave campaign in 2016, served as
Foreign Secretary from 2016 to 2018 and been Prime Minister
since July 2019. What hope was there for backbench MPs?
Anyway, few expected Leave to win the referendum.

Third, the motivations of Leave-supporting Conservative
MPs and many Leave-supporting voters differed. For
Conservative MPs, it was about sovereignty but also about
delivering the next stage of Thatcherism. It was about deregulation, lower taxes, and removing trade barriers (by which they
meant lowering tariffs) with the rest of the world. Britain was
going to be more liberated, more entrepreneurial, more buc-
caneering, freed from the dirigiste tendencies of the EU.

This was not the message conveyed to the electorate by Vote Leave. Leaving meant more money for the NHS and stopping Turkish immigrants. This was not about delivering Singapore-upon-Thames but about going back to a time when we were in 'control'. It was a campaign designed to appeal to those who disliked change and wanted reassurance.

The casualness with which many Conservatives backed Leave, the ignorance of the consequences of leaving and the inconsistency between what the advocates of Brexit wanted and what many of its voters wanted meant that delivering Brexit became immensely difficult and has left many – both MPs and the public – disappointed. This tension between the free market vision of Brexit and the one that many Leave supporters voted for is one that continues to this day and continues to cause tension on the right of British politics.

The rising tide of populism

Our politics appears to be realigning. As Andrew Cooper sets out in Chapter 1, politics is moving away from the politics of economic class – with those who are economically secure voting centre right and those who are insecure voting centre left – towards the politics of culture. Increasingly, a more reliable indicator of how you vote is not your income but your educational background, and the population density and diversity of your neighbourhood.

It has always been the case that the Conservatives have done relatively well with the rural poor and Labour has done relatively well with the urban rich. But in a trend that has been in place for decades, the Conservatives have won increased support in low density, low diversity, relatively poor locations while retreating from relatively prosperous cities. Ex-mining constituencies in the north Midlands, for example, once voted solidly Labour, even with a Conservative landslide. In general election after general election, these areas have swung towards the Conservatives to a greater extent than the national picture would have suggested. In 2019, Labour was almost wiped out in Nottinghamshire, Derbyshire and Staffordshire but for a handful of inner-city constituencies. In contrast, the Conservative performance in London was considerably worse in the 2019 landslide (21 Conservative MPs out of 73) than in 1992 (48 out of 84), when John Major won a small majority.

To some extent, these changes can be put down to economic characteristics. Home ownership is higher outside the big cities, especially London. As James Kanagasooriam, who coined the phrase 'Red Wall', has pointed out, if one looked at the demographic make-up of Red Wall constituencies, the surprising fact was that for many years the Conservatives had underperformed in these areas.[1] The fall of the Red Wall in 2019 was the culmination of many years in which historical ties to Labour (or historical antipathy to the Tories) had weakened.

Nonetheless, the changing geographical distribution of the Conservative vote has changed the nature of political views of Conservative voters. The Tories have retreated in Remain-voting constituencies and advanced in Leave-voting constituencies. The general election of 2019 saw the parliamentary map better reflect the 2016 European referendum. The Conservatives had become, to a much greater extent, the party of Leave.

This came with considerable advantages in the 'first-past-the-post system'. In the 2016 referendum, Remain did well in cities, university towns and Scotland; its vote being heavily concentrated in those areas. The Leave vote was more widely distributed, which meant that, according to analysis done by Chris Hanretty, 409 out of 650 parliamentary constituencies voted Leave, even though Leave only obtained 52 per cent of the vote. The Conservatives also benefited in 2019 by the fact that the Remain vote was split between Labour, Liberal Democrat, Green and, in a handful of cases, Independent plus the nationalist parties in Scotland and Wales. With Nigel Farage's Brexit Party giving sitting Conservative MPs a free run, the Leave vote could rally behind the Tories.

A voting base that leant heavily on Leave voters was not one that embraced the free market vision of Brexit. The 2019 campaign recognised this, with promises of forty new hospitals and 20,000 more police officers. Higher public spending was in order, although little was said about how this was to be funded.

Analysis by UK In a Changing Europe[2] provided a fascinating insight into the views of those who switched from Labour to Conservative for the 2019 general election. These voters were asked various questions that enabled them to be placed on a spectrum on economic values (left to right) and social values (liberal to authoritarian). These switchers were notably to the left of traditional Conservative voters on economic issues but also more socially authoritarian.

There is a temptation to dismiss Johnson's government in 2019 to 2022 as being particularly right wing. It is true to say that on issues such as Brexit and immigration, Johnson sought to govern from the right (although, to be fair, immigration policy for those coming from outside the EU became more liberal) but, taken as a whole, it is more complicated than that. On some issues, Johnson was right wing, on others, such as 'levelling-up', quite left wing. In many respects, one could argue that Johnson's agenda reflected public opinion as whole. Not necessarily coherent and, whether because of Covid or whether because of Johnson's administrative failures, not much was achieved, but one could argue that he fashioned his own type of centre ground. But it was not the politics of the liberal centre right but the politics of populism.

As Rory Stewart writes in Chapter 2, populism is the politics of setting the people versus the elite. This was the approach that Vote Leave pursued in 2016 and it was the approach that Johnson took on becoming Prime Minister in 2019.

Brexit had not been delivered, according to Johnson, not because the Leave campaign had promised the undeliverable (or even that Johnson and his allies had repeatedly voted down a deal that would have delivered Brexit) but because the elite had blocked it.

Remainer ministers and Remainer civil servants had delivered an inadequate deal. Remainer judges ('the enemies of the people') had stood in the way, as had a Remainer parliament, which is why it had to be suspended (not that this was ever explicitly admitted) until the judges (them again) intervened. The people had voted and here we were, more than three years later, still in the EU. It was time to get Brexit done.

It was a clever slogan, appealing not just to diehard Brexiteers but also to those who were tired of the wearisome and prolonged process of leaving the EU. Blame was laid on the elite and their institutions, which had stood in the way of the will of the people. Johnson was presented as the people's tribune, on the people's side, willing to bulldoze through any obstacles to deliver the people's objectives.

It was not a pitch that allowed much room for nuance or subtlety – or, at times, honesty. The inevitable trade-offs involved in governing were dismissed, whether on tax and spend (taxes would be cut, spending increased, borrowing kept under control) or on Brexit. Most egregiously, the government promised that it had a deal on Brexit that would mean no checks on goods crossing the Irish Sea, even though that is exactly what had been agreed.

One particular aspect of the Conservative manifesto was the proposal to reform judicial review. This appeared to have been provoked by the ruling of the Supreme Court that the prorogation of parliament in September 2019 had been unlawful.

Johnson took this badly and wanted to bring the judges down to size. But this reaction was symptomatic of a wider attitude towards the law – that the executive should not be constrained by the judiciary. Laws were for other people.

This manifested itself in a lowering of ethical standards, a common attribute for populists. The Home Secretary, Priti Patel, was allowed to continue in office after being found to have breached the ministerial code (resulting in the resignation of Johnson's first ethics adviser), attempts were made to change the parliamentary standards system to protect Owen Paterson over breached lobbying rules, and a culture of lawbreaking in respect of Covid restrictions was pervasive in 10 Downing Street.

It was also the case that the government considered itself above the application of international law. Having agreed and ratified the Northern Ireland Protocol, the UK was obliged to comply with its terms and, if it wanted to change the terms, do so in accordance with procedures set out in the Protocol. In contrast, during the negotiations of the UK's future relations with the EU, the government announced plans to change unilaterally the terms of the Protocol, with a cabinet minister explicitly stating that the government was going to breach international law, albeit 'in a limited and specific way'.

Eventually, this plan was dropped but the proposal was to return in the form of the Northern Ireland Protocol Bill. At this point, the government argued that it was acting in accordance with international law, albeit few lawyers agreed. Support for the rule of law – including international law – has been a fundamental aspect of mainstream political opinion for a very long time. Margaret Thatcher once declared that the UK's role in the world was to be an advocate for international law. As Dominic Grieve makes clear in Chapter 3, the Johnson government, in particular, failed to meet the standards we should expect.

The extent to which the UK should comply with its international obligations remains a contentious issue for some, particularly in the context of the European Convention on Human Rights (ECHR). For some on the right of British politics, the ECHR imposes unacceptable constraints on the actions a government might want to take, especially in the context of the treatment of asylum seekers. But to leave the ECHR would place the UK in a very small and undesirable club of European nations, alongside Belarus and Russia.

Since its creation in the 1950s (influenced heavily by Conservative politicians), the UK – with the vast majority of democratic European nations – has viewed the ECHR as a buttress to support the rights of the individual and to constrain over mighty governments. Likewise, judicial review has protected the rights of individuals, ensuring that public authorities act reasonably and within their powers. This did not always go without complaints by ministers from all parties but there was recognition that in a modern society, power should be disbursed and checks and balances should be in place. For some on the populist right, this recognition is now contested.

The economy

The dominance of the centre right in UK politics has very largely been based on the British public's view that the Conservatives could be trusted on the economy. Conservatives would be cautious with the public finances, focused on the need to create wealth not just redistribute it, supportive of aspiration, pro-business and practical.

This is not to say that the public thought that the Conservatives got everything right – evidently they did not – but, in comparison with the ideological dogma, trade-union capture and wishful thinking associated with the Labour Party, the Conservatives won the support of the majority of voters who prioritised economic competence. Again, Labour's one period of electoral dominance in modern times coincided with Blair's leadership of Labour when, alongside Gordon Brown, he emphasised New Labour's commitment to aspiration and prudence.

The last few years have proven to be economically turbulent for most Western economies. The Global Financial Crisis hit the UK hard, had a long-term impact on productivity and living standards, and left the public finances fragile and in need of consolidation. By historic standards, growth during 2010–2016 was weak, although, by international standards, as strong as any nation in the G7, as the world economy struggled to recover from a major financial crisis. In 2020, Covid caused an extraordinary recession across the world, with ballooning public debts and, just as the world economy returned to normality, Russia invaded Ukraine. Energy prices surged, living standards fell.

Any government would struggle in those circumstances. The fiscal consolidation following 2010 has received much criticism, although decisive measures to bring down a deficit of eleven per cent of GDP were necessary. Governments cannot hide away from tough decisions and external shocks meant that the country became poorer than we had previously expected. No government could magically change that. There was, however, a policy that was self-inflicted and unnecessary which has done much economic damage. Recognising this and addressing it is essential if the UK is to prosper in future.

The vote to leave the EU on 23 June 2016 caused an immediate and dramatic fall in the pound which, in turn, increased prices and resulted in a fall in living standards. It also created significant uncertainty, which resulted in business investment (which, hitherto, had been growing strongly) to plateau.

As Gavin Barwell shows in Chapter 4, Brexit was always likely to have a negative economic impact. In addition to the initial impact of greater business uncertainty, making it harder to trade with the EU would result in higher prices, lower business investment, lower levels of trade and (as a less open economy and, therefore, less subject to foreign competition) lower levels of productivity.

How economically damaging Brexit would prove was always going to depend upon the nature of Brexit. As Gavin argues, the unwillingness of Conservative Brexiteers to compromise and seek to minimise some of the economic problems caused by our departure from the European Union has meant that the damage has been greater than it might otherwise have been.

This should be a source of great embarrassment to those who advocated Brexit and then opposed those trying to deal with the consequences pragmatically. There are Brexiteers who argue that an economic cost was a price worth paying to 'restore sovereignty' but, at the time of the referendum, warnings of economic detriment were dismissed as 'Project Fear'. A sensible analysis of the British economy and what it needs to improve its lacklustre performance must acknowledge the damage done by erecting trade barriers with our biggest external market and seek to find ways of reducing those barriers.

The challenge for the Conservative Party is to find a way of doing this without losing the support of those who voted Tory because of their enthusiasm for Brexit. In other words, a party that turned itself into the Leave party has to tell Leave voters that it and its supporters were wrong.

This is not just a problem for the Conservative Party. The most contested voters in the most contested constituencies at the next general election are those who switched from Labour to Conservative in 2019. These are, by and large, Leave supporters and the Labour Party will tread very carefully to avoid offending them. It appears unlikely that either party will acknowledge the obvious economic truth about the consequences of leaving the EU, especially with the thin trade deal that we now have.

The liberal centre right voice has been largely excluded from this debate. Defeated in the referendum, it was the Brexit ultras that prevailed in the long years the followed. Attempts at a compromise deal by Theresa May (which was hardly a 'soft Brexit' compared to some of the promises made by Brexiteers in 2016) were thwarted by a combination of those who wanted no Brexit and those who wanted a very hard Brexit. Johnson's general election triumph of 2019 meant that we got the very hard Brexit. Those of us who warned about the consequences have been vindicated. Indeed, the combination of the pandemic (which involved many EU migrants returning home and many UK citizens retiring early) and Brexit has resulted in even more damage to the UK labour market than might have been expected.

The centre right of British politics can face up to the economic realities or it can continue to live in a state of denial. If it chooses the latter, it is hard to see how its reputation for economic competence can be fully restored. Brexit's impact on economic thinking within the centre right has had a wider impact than being on the wrong side of one of the biggest economic issues of the age. It has also led to scepticism, even downright hostility, from the right towards economic expertise.

This was most apparent during the brief and disastrous premiership of Liz Truss in the autumn of 2022. Truss, and her Chancellor of the Exchequer, Kwasi Kwarteng, wanted to cut taxes in the belief that this would result in higher economic growth. It was their belief that the UK had been held back by the 'Treasury orthodoxy' and 'abacus economics' that questioned whether tax cuts for the rich necessarily paid for themselves.

The mini-Budget of Friday, 23 September 2022 tested this thinking to destruction. The bond markets could not see how Kwarteng's strategy made fiscal or political sense, especially in a climate when interest rates were already going up to counter inflation. The pound fell, gilt yields rose. That was on the Friday, giving ministers the chance to take stock and use the weekend to reassure the markets that no further risks would be taken. Instead, the Chancellor briefed the Sunday papers and used a Sunday morning television interview to assert his determination to cut taxes further. Once the markets re-opened, the foolishness of this approach was revealed, as the pound sank to a record low against the dollar.

The government's position was not helped by the fact that, in the days running up to the mini-Budget, it had gone out of its way to undermine the UK's economic institutions. The respected Permanent Secretary to the Treasury, Sir Tom Scholar, had been sacked by Kwarteng on the Chancellor's first day in office. The OBR, which would normally have set out a forecast of the public finances alongside the policy announcements, was excluded from the process. And, during the Conservative Party leadership campaign, the role of an independent Bank of England in setting interest rates had been questioned by Truss's campaign.

Institutions – vital in establishing trust – were undermined, expertise questioned. Truss was not a populist like Johnson (she positively revelled in advocating policies she thought right but unpopular), but she shared the populists' instinct for dismissing evidence that was inconvenient and contrary to her prejudices. The Truss world-view was a caricature of Thatcherism. Whereas Thatcher was, in reality, cautious and fiscally conservative (she was prepared to raise taxes and only engaged in net tax cuts when the public finances were strong), Truss wanted to jump straight to the exciting, tax-cutting stage of governing without building up credibility and strong public finances in the interim. It did not impress the markets, the public or her MPs. Her premiership was the shortest in British history.

The Conservative reputation for economic competence was left in tatters. A period of Johnsonian incoherence was followed by Trussite ideology. It was left to Rishi Sunak and Jeremy Hunt to pick up the pieces and at least restore some market credibility, even if their Tory critics accused them of uninspiring managerialism.

If the centre right is to re-establish its economic reputation, it has to break away from populism and faux Thatcherism. As

Tim Pitt argues in Chapter 5, there is a broader, centre right and Conservative inheritance that should be brought to the fore. This means facing up to the realities of our economy and the trade-offs that apply. Changing expectations and demography will increase pressure on public spending and this cannot be wished away. Growth is necessary but we cannot afford to engage in wishful thinking and the belief that deregulation and tax cuts will have magical impacts. And society has changed since the 1980s and inequality is not an issue that can be ignored.

Public services matter. Valuing public services should not be seen as a monopoly of the left. This means not just funding public services properly but also ensuring value for money, delivering reform and putting the consumers of public services first. As Anne Milton explains in Chapter 6, the NHS is a priority issue for the public and it is vital that the centre right restores trust in its commitment to it. It is also, of course, vital that we have a growing economy to pay for rising expectations of our public services.

On the subject of growth, it is widely recognised that science and technology will play an important part. The UK has many advantages in these sectors but we cannot afford to be complacent. In Chapter 7, Sam Gyimah sets out a compelling, liberal, centre right agenda on how the UK can succeed. At a time of great economic uncertainty, the loss of a strong liberal centre right voice leaves the UK vulnerable. For the most part, the left struggles to suppress its anti-business and anti-aspiration instincts; the populist right has little interest in or understanding of what makes a modern economy work; and the free market ideologues have proven themselves unwilling to face up to the real world. A return to liberal centre right economic values is overdue.

Internationalism

There are two aspects of the populist right which commonly appear across the world – short termism and scepticism about science. In many countries, not least the US, this has resulted in the rejection of the science of climate change and, as a consequence, an unwillingness to pay even a small price to address it.

As Amber Rudd notes in Chapter 8, this approach has not become dominant on the right of British politics (Johnson's UK government engaged heavily in chairing COP 26) but there remain voices in the right of British politics ready to oppose taking adequate measures to mitigate climate change.

The liberal centre right should be forward-thinking and long-termist. This means facing up to the challenges of climate change and threats to bio-diversity.

These are not matters of concern only to the elite, a concern of the comfortable middle classes faced with relatively few immediate worries. Opinion polling consistently shows that climate change ranks as a priority issue for a large proportion of the population, across generations and social classes.

This is not, however, how some on the right see it. We should be wary of the divisive 'them and us' rhetoric that can too easily apply to this subject in which concern for the environment is portrayed as being hostile to the interests of ordinary people and advocated by out-of-touch globalists. Were such an approach to become common-place on the right of British politics, it would be damaging both to the cause of tackling climate change (creating an uncertain business investment environment, for example) but also inflict long-term reputational damage on the right who, in all likelihood, would find themselves on the wrong side of history.

Why the liberal centre right remains necessary

This is a book that does not shy away from criticising the decisions and behaviour of Conservative governments and politicians. Powerful short-term electoral considerations combined with political opportunism resulted in the Conservatives moving away from liberal values, and the country has paid a price.

Over time, a political party that has increasingly relied on socially authoritarian, less educated voters born before 1960 is likely to struggle with an electorate that is increasingly socially liberal and more educated. The consequence may be that the centre right as a whole becomes increasingly irrelevant, tarnished by its association with populism and a Brexit experiment which – particularly in the eyes of younger people – is seen to have failed. While the book makes the case against populism, it also makes the positive case that the centre right (albeit a liberal, outward-looking one) must once again be a powerful force.

Few politicians have represented the values of the liberal centre right as boldly or achieved as much over the last fifty years as Michael Heseltine. Even in his tenth decade, Michael's passion is undiminished and in Chapter 9 he presents a forward-looking agenda for restoring the UK's fortunes and place in the world. With vast experience of government, he makes the case for much greater engagement with the EU and a willingness to embrace devolution within the UK.

As Daniel Finkelstein sets out in the concluding chapter, the country benefits from centrist politics in which trade-offs are evaluated, complexity grappled with and compromise is accepted. Where the centre right differs from the centre left is as much one of temperament as ideology. On government borrowing, social reform, constitutional change and the role of international institutions, the centre right is more cautious, sceptical and, as often as not, more realistic than the centre left. That caution and realism has spared the country from error and, when persuaded to embrace change, ensured that any such change is secure and longstanding.

Much of this book focuses on how pragmatic centrism fell out of fashion within the Conservative Party. But it must also be acknowledged that the position of centrists within the Labour Party has often been fragile. The history of the Labour Party makes clear that the forces dragging it away from the centre ground and towards dogmatic and impractical policies are very strong. Jeremy Corbyn may no longer be a Labour MP but the forces that made him leader of the Labour Party have not entirely disappeared.

We live under a 'first-past-the-post' system, which tends towards a two-party system. It is possible that Labour will one day transform itself into a party defined by its commitment to open and liberal values (as some would argue happened under Blair's leadership) but the overwhelming likelihood is that it will always be a party of the left – even if not of the far left, as it was as recently as 2019.

That leaves the Conservative Party, the traditional home for the liberal centre right, in coalition with other traditions of the right. The case made in this book is that the Conservative Party has moved away from the liberal aspect of its traditions. Most – but not all – of the authors, however, would argue that, under the current electoral system, the most straightforward manner in which the liberal centre right can be revived is for the Conservatives to change course, recognise that the embrace of populism has been a mistake and reinvent itself to appeal to new generations of supporters. The Conservative Party, after all, has been capable of reinvention in the past.

The power of the party membership, which appears to have moved strongly to the right in recent years, will make such a reinvention challenging. It would require large numbers of liberal-minded people to put aside their reservations about the Conservative Party and join it, allowing them to influence the choice of party candidates and, in due course, the party leadership. Recent history suggests that Conservative leadership elections are never very far off. A general election defeat in 2024 would very probably precipitate another one.

Recapturing the Conservative Party may be the most straightforward manner of re-establishing the influence of the liberal centre right but it would also be fair to say that there is no guarantee that the next transformation of the Conservative Party will be in the correct direction. In the months and years ahead, there is likely to be a robust debate about where the Conservative Party should go next and we hope that this book will give encouragement to those arguing for a sustained return to a more liberal position. If that endeavour proves to be unsuccessful, the liberal centre right will face some stark choices. In the meantime, those who share our approach should seek to come together, continue to articulate our values, and prepare for whatever the future may hold.

Part of that project is this book. It is not a manifesto of policies and not every contributor will agree with every word set out within it. Where we are all in agreement is that, whatever happens with the Conservative Party, the UK needs a strong and powerful liberal centre right. It was a force in British politics that more often than not dominated government either in directly providing the nation's leadership or, on those relatively rare circumstances when not holding power, exerting strong influence on that nation's leadership.

At its best, the liberal centre right provided stability and security. It protected and enhanced our institutions; it respected the rule of law. It encouraged economic openness and innovation, helping to deliver increased prosperity. It widened opportunity and supported aspiration, allowing a greater proportion of society to live fulfilling and enriched lives. And it welcomed and nurtured social progress, making us a more civilised and tolerant nation.

The liberal centre right has been in retreat in recent years and, in every sense, the country is the poorer for it. But, if anything, the failures of the populist right make the case powerfully for why we need to return to the values of openness, internationalism, moderation, prudence and integrity. It is time to make the case for the liberal centre right once again.

1

The Realignment of British Politics

Andrew Cooper

Famously, there was a sign at the top of the stairs in the war room of Bill Clinton's 1992 presidential campaign headquarters. Put there by his irascible campaign manager James Carville, it was intended to serve as a constant reminder to the campaign staff of what the election was all about: 'The economy, stupid.' The phrase quickly became a political cliché. It seemed to be a truism – capturing the essence of what, more than anything else, determined how most people voted, explaining the central story of elections in the post-war era.

As a crude shorthand for understanding the core of party support, Carville's phrase could be applied to the UK too. Reflecting this country's particular history and neuroses, the structure of party support was often defined more in terms of social class than economic position and outlook, but the essential story was the same.

There was a consistent pattern in post-war elections. The Labour Party's demographic core was people with lower incomes and blue-collar jobs: the working class (technically defined, in the clunky, occupation-based coding of the market research world, as socio-economic groups C2, D and E). The Conservative Party's demographic core was people with higher incomes and white-collar jobs; the middle class (A, B and C1, in the same research-sector parlance).

As the British Election Study[1] summarised in 2019, the 'fundamental structure' of British politics was that 'the vast majority of the working class' voted Labour and the 'vast majority of the middle class' backed the Tories. Each party routinely won elections by margins of 30 per cent or more in these respective heartlands and the governments they formed were built on those demographic foundations.

At their most successful, of course, both Labour and the Conservatives succeeded in reaching well beyond their economically defined core vote. The Tories in 1983 and 1987 and then Labour in 1997 and 2001 won landslides by also winning outside their traditional core. Nevertheless, they were building on that traditional economic base; the foundation remained the dominance of their established economic heartlands. The economic situation and demographic profile of the average Conservative voter was, therefore, more or less the same in 1983 and in 1997, respectively the biggest Tory landslide since 1924 and the heaviest Tory defeat since 1832. There were, obviously, a lot fewer Tory voters in 1997 than in 1983, but in terms of their average economic profile, they were very alike.

In the years since the New Labour triumph in 1997, the picture has changed radically. It has become increasingly clear that the main driver of voting is no longer just 'the economy, stupid'. The axis of politics has rotated significantly, fundamentally disrupting the demographic structure of party support. The Brexit referendum of 2016 and the results of the two general elections in the subsequent three years made this unmistakably clear. Factors that were nothing to do with economic position and outlook had plainly become significant drivers of who people voted for. Culture, identity and social values were exerting a growing influence on voting behaviour. A person's educational background, feelings on cultural issues and the diversity of the community they live in were becoming at least as important as their economic situation in shaping their political priorities and attitudes.

Open vs. closed

Tony Blair was the first political leader to see this and to describe in clear terms the nature of the structural political realignment that was underway. Speaking in 2006 – a full decade before the vote for Brexit made the realignment glaringly obvious – he noted that 'there is a debate going on, which confusingly for the politicians often crosses traditional left/right economic lines. The debate is "open" versus "closed".'[2]

What Tony Blair identified was that the key battle line dividing the UK into two broad political tribes was ceasing to be characterised by voter attitudes on the left/right spectrum of economic issues and becoming ever more defined by people's reaction to the social and cultural consequences of globalisation. The world was opening up and becoming ever faster; borders were loosening; cultures were blending; national sovereignty was becoming more contingent. The upheaval was immense and powerful. Many people's response was to welcome these changes, to embrace them and to see them as, fundamentally, the opening up of new opportunities. Many others had the opposite reaction, seeing these winds of change as threatening and unsettling, and wanting to try to shut out as much of the impact as possible. These two, opposing worldviews – respectively 'open' and 'closed' – were starting to exert a strong influence on who people voted for, regardless of their economic situation.

This rotation of the political axis is not just happening in the UK. The same structural shift is evident in numerous Western democracies. The extent of the disruption to voting patterns and parties varies depending on national and regional factors as well as electoral systems. But the same general story has been playing out in, to cite a few examples, the United States, France, Italy, Germany and Scandinavia: the rising salience of cultural factors and identity politics among particular demographic groups causing political parties to shift ground as they try to respond to a different agenda and to a growth in populism on both the left and the right, which has also been spawned by the rotation of the axis.

At the time, the Brexit referendum and the aftershock of the Trump victory a few months later – and the significance in these results of cultural factors and identity politics – felt like quite an abrupt disturbance of established drivers of voting behaviour. Now, looking back with hindsight, the 'open' vs. 'closed' divide has been increasingly visible in the entrails of elections, at least since 1997.

This pattern can be seen, for example, in the composition of Labour's vote as it started to decline from its high watermark of 44 per cent in 1997. Labour had won a majority of nearly 200 seats promising that 'a new day has dawned'; their soundtrack was 'Things can only get better.' Hopes were impossibly high. Inevitably, as the months and years passed, some people who had voted Labour started to feel disappointed and switched their support away from Labour to other parties. But, rather than happening fairly evenly across different voter types, the erosion of Labour's 1997 vote had a very particular skew. The people who voted Labour in 1997 but then in 2001, 2005 or 2010 voted for another party were disproportionately those on lower incomes and with fewer qualifications;[3] those who were the party's traditional core. More strikingly still, they were very disproportionately people who in the UK census defined their national identity as 'English' rather than 'British'. Very disproportionately, when the time came years later, they voted in favour of the UK leaving the European Union. Culture and identity politics significantly shifted the centre of gravity of Labour's demographic coalition between 1997 and 2010.

In the four elections preceding the Brexit referendum, the Conservative Party's demographic coalition was changing too. The average Tory voter was becoming steadily less well off and less well educated. The Conservatives were losing ground in urban areas; population density and diversity were increasingly important factors in party support, while economic status was becoming less of a predictor of voting.

The Brexit referendum undoubtedly accelerated this shift in the geology and geography of UK politics. But the social and cultural fault-line that Brexit exposed had in fact been there, widening and growing in significance, for years. On 23 June 2016, the question on the ballot paper was whether the UK should remain in the EU or leave it. But, for most people on both sides of the argument – even if they weren't necessarily conscious of the fact – the Brexit question went much deeper. It was a proxy for their core social and political values; a signal of their world view.

We know this because reams of poll data align on the extremely strong relationship between the way people voted in the 2016 referendum and their stance on a range of social and cultural questions. Someone, for example, with a strongly positive view overall on the impact on the UK of immigration, multiculturalism, globalisation, feminism and the Green movement was overwhelmingly likely also to vote for the UK to Remain in the EU. Someone with a firmly negative view on these issues was extremely likely to vote for Brexit.

Support for Brexit also aligned closely with authoritarian attitudes on numerous social and cultural questions, which were ostensibly unrelated to the question of EU membership – just as liberal attitudes on those questions tended to coincide with support for remaining in the EU. Feelings about national sovereignty are for most people, in other words, shaped by a world view and core values, rather than by pragmatic considerations. How people felt about the impact of globalisation and its cultural as well as economic consequences was more important in the Brexit referendum than how people felt about either the general principles or the policy specifics of the UK's relationship with the European Union.

This is why the Brexit referendum was so divisive and polarising, why the division has proved so enduring and (especially for those who have been part of the Conservative Party's coalition) politically defining and why so relatively few people have changed their mind. The Remain/Leave question cut vastly deeper than the proximate question of what the UK's relations should be with the EU.

The previous three decades had been characterised by extraordinarily rapid change. The world had both opened-up and speeded-up to an unprecedented degree. Globalisation brought intense economic pressures as well as opportunities; the exportation of many jobs and the extinction of others. Traditional industries shrank in scale, or folded altogether, stripping communities of their economic heart and even their sense of dignity. It became increasingly hard to earn a reasonable living without skills and qualifications relevant to the modern economy.

The opening up of borders accelerated the flow of economic migration, changing both the cultural complexion of the country and the dynamics of the labour market. Multiculturalism became a fact of life, transforming communities. Rapid growth in huge countries on the other side of the world, combined with the internet revolution, tilted the balance of both economic and political power. The UK's sovereignty was increasingly diluted and pooled, diminishing our ability to stand alone. Many people, entirely reasonably, felt both economically and culturally vulnerable. And, crucially, it felt that they had never been consulted on these changes; that nobody had voted for any of it.

Furthermore, through recession in the 1980s, boom in the 1990s, the financial crash and then austerity, for millions of people real living standards stagnated or declined. People were not imagining that their lives were harder, that their quality of life was poorer and their futures more difficult – those were realities. But it did not feel that we were all in it together; some people seemed to be prospering from the same waves of change that were undermining the security and prospects of others, opening the door to the populism that Rory Stewart describes in Chapter 2.

At the same time, public services seemed increasingly, in many parts of the country, to be buckling under the pressure and it was easy to blame this on too rapid a flow of immigration. A large majority of people (including some who were relatively relaxed about the cultural implications of high levels of immigration) were dismayed at the idea of people who had, as they saw it, never put anything into our country, coming to the UK and immediately drawing on its public services and social support systems.

Many people, especially older generations, felt further unsettled because of cultural changes driven by rapid social liberalisation. 'I hardly recognise my country, anymore' was the sum of these factors for many. Those who agreed with that statement overwhelmingly voted to leave the EU. This was not in any sense a uniquely British phenomenon. The same feelings were playing out in very similar ways in numerous developed economies, as the opening-up of world markets and the rapid growth of previously less developed economies disrupted the established political order in country after country.

As the Venezuelan writer and commentator (and former Trade Minister) Moisés Naim observed in his brilliant book *The Revenge of Power*, in numerous different countries the same pattern could be observed: 'new identity groups form around a burning sense of grievance. They're brought together by the very real experience of being left behind economically, disrespected culturally and immersed in an increasingly alien-seeming, threatening society. It is these groups, propelled by status dissonance, that are creating political instability on an unprecedented scale in political systems around the globe.'[4]

The politics of nostalgia

Against this background, the Vote Leave slogan 'Take Back Control' struck a deep emotional chord with many people. It was a brilliant (if cynical) insight, informed by huge amounts of opinion research, that the sum of all the unsettling change in the world was, for millions of voters, a feeling of loss of 'control' – for them in their own lives and for the UK in the world. Their reaction was to want to insulate themselves and their communities from the turbulent global forces.

While the word 'Control' in the Vote Leave slogan had great emotional impact, it is important also to note that the word 'back' carried a lot of weight too. It is there very deliberately to stir nostalgia for a past era, which many remembered (or misremembered) as safer, simpler, stronger and more stable, and which they would love to go 'back' to. Polling during the referendum campaign found that many of the staunchest supporters of Brexit also agreed strongly that 'if I could wave a magic wand and take Britain back to the 1950s, I would'.

This evocation of a better past is a well-established campaign trope. Ronald Reagan's evocative and powerful 1984 re-election slogan is often mis-remembered as 'Morning In America'. In fact, it was 'Morning Again in America'. The word 'again' is serving the same function as the word 'back' in the Vote Leave slogan. The same, of course, applied to Trump's 'Make America Great *Again*'. The American political analyst Yuval Levin points out that this tendency towards political nostalgia afflicts both the left and right of politics, each referencing different moments from the past that supposedly represent the acme of a country's political, economic and social development, according to their respective political narrative.

Progress in this way often becomes defined by both sides as recovery of what that earlier, supposedly golden, age had to offer. This tilts countries in the wrong direction. As Levin notes, it causes people to think of the current era of profound transformation and uncertainty 'not so much as a *transition*, but as an *aberration*'. This mistake leads politicians to focus on – and frame their response to public policy challenges around – the idea of a return to a normal, better, previous, formula, rather than by focusing on the world as it is now and responding positively to today's challenges. It is a tempting route for politicians to follow because it enables them to avoid facing up to uncomfortable new realities and implies that there are tried and tested paths available to deal with what otherwise often seem intimidating policy challenges.

The point about the past times that people hanker for is that, even if they are not romanticised misremembrance (which they usually are), they were as Yuval Levin notes, 'made possible by a set of circumstances – historical, social, economic, political, and cultural – that are no longer with us. These circumstances constituted an inevitably fleeting transition . . . No combination of public policies could recreate them. No amount of moral hectoring will either.'[5] To put this back into the context of Brexit, we can't, in other words, recreate the degree of control – over our individual lives or our standing as a country – that applied in bygone decades, because the macro conditions have utterly changed.

By framing the Brexit referendum as being about taking *back* control, the Leave campaign effectively positioned the outcome as simply being the undoing of changes that had made people feel vulnerable – about their place in the economy and society and the UK's place in the world. There was never any clarity, or remotely a consensus, about what Brexit did, or should, mean in practice; indeed, there still isn't, nearly seven years later and more than three years after the UK finally exited the EU. It was Margaret Thatcher who pointed out, during the first referendum on Europe, in 1975, that 'there is not a genuine alternative' to UK membership.[6]

The reality is that most of those who voted to leave the EU weren't voting *for* an alternative vision of the UK's relationship with the European Union and globally. They were voting *against* the way that the world – and the UK's place in it – had been so rapidly and radically transformed.

When Tony Blair framed the emerging political dichotomy as 'open vs. closed' he noted that the question flowing from this was 'Do we embrace the challenge of more open societies, or do we build defences against it?' It is very clear that for most people a vote for Brexit was an expression of the wish to build defences against the consequences of an open world; it was a vote for 'closed'.

Many Tory Brexiteers would no doubt strenuously reject the characterisation of their position as 'closed'. Some would claim that their post-Brexit vision was the opposite – 'global Britain'; a United Kingdom freed from the sclerotic bureaucracy of the European Union and liberated to thrive in the wider global economy by the competitive advantages of less regulation, lower tax and a smaller state. This was quite possibly the ideal that attracted some Conservatives to support Brexit. But it was absolutely not the story of Brexit that was presented to the British public.

There may be many reasons why so many of today's champions of 'global Britain' ('Singapore-on-Thames' in their common shorthand) chose not to share that vision with voters before the referendum. For one thing, not all of the Tory campaigners for Brexit agreed with it and some of the few Labour figures in Vote Leave strongly disagreed. In any case, a strategic decision had been taken not to get drawn into debate about what 'Leave' would actually mean in practice; it was much easier to persuade people to vote *against* the EU than in favour of a particular alternative arrangement. But it is undoubtedly also true that the vision of a low-tax, small-state, lightly regulated post-Brexit 'global Britain' had very little support with the electorate. If Vote Leave had made that argument, they would surely have lost.

Opposing campaigns always test the strengths and weaknesses of each other's arguments. When the Remain campaign conducted polling – many months before the referendum – to test the popularity of different iterations of what the Leave narrative might be, it found that at most only fifteen per cent of voters were attracted to a 'global Britain' picture of life for the UK outside the EU. The Director of the Vote Leave campaign Dominic Cummings reached the same conclusion. In a detailed analysis a few months after the referendum, he noted that while the 'Go Global' argument was 'a firm favourite for many years among a subset of MPs and Farage's inner circle' it was 'a total loser with the public'.[7]

The case made for Brexit was – with careful intent – a psychologically compelling appeal to 'closed' values. The core arguments were that leaving the EU would enable the UK to take back control of its borders and that Brexit would repatriate £350m a week, which would go to the NHS instead of Brussels. The UK would regain absolute national sovereignty; only laws made by the UK parliament would have any jurisdiction. There was also a lot invested in specific scaremongering about the prospect of Turkey ('population 76 million') joining the EU – with a leaflet highlighting Syria and Iraq as Turkey's neighbours. It is difficult to imagine a more brazen and emotive appeal to 'closed' values.

The big lie of Cakeism

A few prominent Brexit advocates did say during the campaign that leaving the EU would (and should) mean leaving the single market. But most either avoided the question, or insisted that after a vote for Brexit, the UK would stay in the single market; that the strength of our negotiating position meant that the EU would have no option but to concede this; that the bosses of major EU-based exporters would force their political leaders to go along with it. Many times during the referendum campaign, the confident assurance that we would retain membership of the single market was deployed in order to undercut the claimed risks of leaving the EU. Unsurprisingly given who was leading it, the consistent narrative of the Leave campaign was that we could have our cake and eat it.

The effectiveness of this approach could be seen clearly in the poll data. When voters were asked during the referendum campaign what they thought the most likely outcome would be if the UK voted for Brexit, consistently less than a quarter thought that leaving the EU would mean losing access to the single market. A similar number thought that if the referendum result was a majority for Leave, the UK would end up staying in the EU anyway – because the EU would panic and come back with vastly improved terms to persuade us not to leave. But most people – consistently more than half – thought that if a majority voted for Brexit, then the UK would leave the EU, but would retain access to the single market and other benefits of membership. The Leave campaign did not persuade people that it was worth losing access to the single market in order to gain the benefits of not being in the EU. They persuaded people, entirely falsely, that we would never be faced with that trade-off at all.

Boris Johnson continued to assert this even after the referendum. In his column in *The Daily Telegraph* four days after the vote (and a few weeks before he started to insist that staying in the single market, or even a customs union, would, in fact, be a betrayal of Brexit), he wrote that 'British people will still be able to go and work in the EU; to live; to travel; to study; to buy homes and to settle down . . . There will continue to be free trade, and access to the single market.'[8]

Churchill famously described how in April 1917, Lenin, 'the most grisly of weapons', was sent by Germany back to Russia to foment chaos, 'transported in a sealed truck, like a plague bacillus'. In a similar way, Boris Johnson was transported in a red bus, touring disempowered parts of the UK, contaminating them with specious, populist, 'cake-ite' boosterism.

Volte face

The reason why it is important to look at the Brexit referendum in such detail is because belief in Brexit became, almost overnight, the Conservative Party's defining conviction – often it has seemed, its *raison d'être*. This was a violent deviation from the longstanding belief system of the Tory party. Almost from the moment that the idea was conceived of establishing formal structures to bring European nations closer together, developing common policies on key issues, the Conservative Party was in favour of it and wanted the UK to be part of it. As Margaret Thatcher put it, the Tories had been 'pursuing the European dream almost as long as we have existed as a party'.[9]

When the original six member states signed the Treaty of Rome in 1957, establishing the European Economic Community and customs union, the Conservative Prime Minister Harold Macmillan soon came to the view that Britain should join it too. This became the defining mission of the Conservative government he led and it was his Tory government that submitted the formal application to join the EEC in 1961. From then on, belief in 'Europe' and support for the UK being at the heart of it was an unwavering and defining position of the Conservative Party and often a key dividing line between the Tories and Labour, who were first opposed (under Gaitskell), then ambivalent (under Wilson), then opposed again (under Foot and Kinnock), before eventually, in the 1990s becoming enthusiastically positive.

In the highly charged House of Commons vote on the motion to apply for accession to the European Community in October 1972, 77 per cent of Labour MPs voted against and 89 per cent of Conservative MPs voted in favour. When, in April 1975, the House of Commons held a free vote on whether or not the UK should stay in the EC, 91 per cent of Conservative MPs voted in favour. Tory MPs were much more strongly pro-Europe than the country as a whole.

Six weeks after that vote in parliament, the UK voted by a
2 to 1 margin in favour of remaining in the EC ('the Common
Market' as it was also described on the ballot paper). In that
first referendum on membership, 88 per cent of Conservative
supporters voted to stay in, compared with 58 per cent of
Labour voters.[10] The historian Dominic Sandbrook notes in
his account of the period that 'it was the Tories who provided the backbone of the official Yes campaign'.[11] It was the
Conservative Party's political machine that was 'handing out
the leaflets, booking speakers, organising rallies and getting
out the vote on referendum day'. By a strange coincidence,
the number of votes in the 1975 referendum for staying in was
identical to the number of votes in the 2016 referendum for
getting out: 17.4 million.

Taking the UK into membership of the European
Community was the principal (and arguably the only) major
achievement of Edward Heath's government – a second successive Tory administration for which this was the defining
mission. In the 1983 and 1987 general elections, when withdrawal from Europe was a central plank in Labour's election
manifesto, this was cited by Conservatives – not least Margaret
Thatcher – as clear evidence of their unfitness to govern. The
European single market was a British Conservative idea and its
achievement was one of the central defining missions of the
Thatcher government.

For more than sixty years, support for what eventually
became the European Union was the orthodox mainstream
position of the Conservative Party. Even in her famous Bruges
speech, Margaret Thatcher stressed that 'Britain does not
dream of some cosy, isolated existence on the fringes of the
European Community. Our destiny is in Europe, as part of the
Community.'[12] Scepticism about the trajectory of the EU and
the costs of this to the UK plainly grew in scale and volume
throughout the period of the Major government and the New
Labour years that followed it. But almost no one in the Tory

Party ever ventured the view that the UK should contemplate leaving the EU.

When the dominant force in politics was 'the economy, stupid', most Conservatives agreed on most of the important aspects of the debate – and tended to disagree with Labour on most of them. There was not unanimity within the Conservative Party on these things, but there was a broad and stable consensus among Tories in support of fiscal responsibility ('sound money' as the Thatcherites would have said), keeping taxes as low as prudence allowed and the importance of encouraging and rewarding entrepreneurship. The rotation of the political axis made these economic dimensions of traditional Conservative Party consensus less salient and pulled into the political agenda a set of issues related to culture and identity, on which the Tory Party is much more divided, creating a bandwagon within the party for an ever-harder line on the EU.

Becoming a single-issue party

By the time of the 2016 referendum, this divide was deep. A significant majority (58%) of people who had voted Conservative at the general election a year earlier backed Leave. But it bears emphasis that a very substantial minority (42%) voted Remain.[13] This equates to five million people voting Conservative at the 2015 general election and then Remain in the referendum a year later. A year after the referendum, when Theresa May called an election to seek a mandate – and a bigger parliamentary majority – for her approach to Brexit, the proportion of Tory voters who had voted Remain dropped to 25 per cent. Two years later, when Boris Johnson called another election to 'Get Brexit Done', this proportion had dropped to less than twenty per cent. The sum of this is that between 2015 and 2019 the Conservatives lost the support of nearly three million people who had voted for Remain.

Brexit divided the traditional support of both the main political parties and they responded in different ways. Labour opted
to fudge the issue – to try to hold onto both its strongly Remain
flank of younger, more diverse, urban people with liberal social
values, and its staunchly pro-Brexit wing of older, less well-
educated, poorer people with conservative social values. The
Conservatives, by contrast, allowed themselves to be redefined
by Brexit. They became, instantly, a Brexit party. There was
an easy logic to this decision. Not only had most Tory voters
been pro-Brexit, but three-quarters of Conservative-held seats
in parliament had majorities for Leave. Remain won in only 81
Conservative-held constituencies, and in only 63 of these was
there a majority *of Tory voters* for Remain. Furthermore, Tory
activists were even more strongly for Brexit than Tory voters.

As the Conservative Party became virtually a single-issue
party of Brexit in the weeks and months that followed the
referendum, they began, in effect, to trade away Tory voters
(many of them very longstanding) who had voted Remain in
favour of Brexit supporters who had previously voted Labour
(in many cases, for generations).

As the argument raged about what Brexit actually meant in
practice, Britain became more deeply polarised and the central Tory position grew more hardline. In tone, language and
substance, the Tory government started to look and sound like
English nationalists, rather than Conservative and Unionists.
Anything and everything, it seemed, could be cast aside in
the pursuit of Brexit at any cost. Not only hardline fringe
figures but senior ministers and advisers at the heart of the
Tory government signalled that a 'no deal Brexit' could be
desirable; that getting Brexit concluded as soon as possible was
more important than peace in Ireland; that it would be worth
Scotland leaving the UK if that was the price of getting Brexit
done; that the pursuit of a hard Brexit justified the trashing
of institutions and the breaking of international law. In the
context of a country where for every seventeen people who

had voted to Leave, sixteen people had voted to Remain, the extremism of the party's stance on Brexit alienated millions, including growing numbers of people who had previously been in the Conservative coalition.

Moisés Naim has identified '3 Ps' that politicians deploy to undermine democracy: populism, polarisation and post-truth. They are not the preserve of left or right. Jeremy Corbyn and others on the extremist left utilise these techniques. Trump and Orbán do. In the UK, the Conservative Party has dabbled, at least, with all three in its attempt to 'get Brexit done' at any price.

'Populism', in Naim's definition, is not an ideology, but a 'poisonous frame': the portrayal of 'the basic fault line in society as the conflict between a corrupt elite and a virtuous, long-suffering people'.[14] We can all recall Conservative politicians campaigning for Brexit, and defending it after the referendum, on exactly those lines. Michael Gove's infamous, shameful, comment that 'the people of this country have had enough of experts from organisations with acronyms, saying they know what is best' came straight from this populist playbook.

'Polarisation' is the deliberate intent to heighten, rather than cool, political tensions by, in Moisés Naim's words, 'turning any and every political discussion into a referendum on one thing: are you on the side of the righteous people, or are you on the side of the rotten, voracious elite?'

As it has become ever clearer that the Brexit they promised is a mirage – that the benefits of Brexit, which they confidently promised, don't exist and will never exist – Conservative politicians have, in desperation, started to become practitioners of 'post-truth'. This term, as Moisés Naim encapsulates it, does not refer to the tendency of most politicians at least some of the time to lie, but the much more insidious distortion of the terms of debate 'to such an extreme that people lose sight of the distinction between truth and lies'. This is more or less a character note on Boris Johnson, but it is what numerous other Tory politicians are doing when they brush away facts about the growing cost of Brexit as 'Remoanerism' or 'project fear'. Notably, Liz Truss used the same technique during her leadership contest with Rishi Sunak, to bat away his entirely accurate warnings of the dire consequences of her profound economic illiteracy.

The American writer and politician Daniel Patrick Moynihan coined one of the most important ground-rules of democratic politics: everyone is entitled to their own opinion, but not to their own facts. This should not be a controversial principle to respect. The Conservative Party used to prize its rooting in the real world; it was core to the party's identity that its approach was grounded in cautious reality; it moved on the basis of rationality, evidence, facts. It was sceptical of grand visions, utopian ideologies and leaps of faith. In the adoption of Brexit as its defining belief, today's Tories have swept all of that away.

With each of these steps, the Conservative Party has been following the gravitational pull of the shifting demographic structure of politics. Tories have opted to follow the line of least resistance, rather than developing a strong, outward-looking and positive agenda to respond to the new challenges and opportunities of a much more open world.

As culture, identity and social values became ever more salient in how voters evaluated parties, for very many voters Brexit position became the shorthand for where people stood more broadly on these issues. Most voters are still more likely to define their own political positioning by reference to their 2016 referendum vote – as either a 'Remainer' or a 'Leaver' – than by their affinity to any political party.

The Conservative rallying call at the 2019 election to 'Get Brexit done' pulled together a coalition built fundamentally on culture and identity politics. Tony Blair noted that 'it consists of some who see Brexit as the facilitator of a new, reforming, global Britain; and others, notably in the old Labour seats of the North, who see Brexit as allowing us to return to the nation "we once were". One is small "r" radical; the other small "c" conservative.'[15]

While these two groups of voters aligned on Brexit – albeit often for different reasons – and on other issues of cultural values, they differed significantly in their economic situation outlook. This is a significant strategic problem for the Conservatives and means that they will have to continue to rely on cultural dividing lines to hold together and animate their post-referendum demographic coalition. The momentum of the realignment of our politics will continue to pull the Tories away from their historic economically defined electoral base.

One demographic dimension in particular is of existential importance for the Conservative Party: age. It is well understood that in 2016 younger people voted heavily for Remain, while older people voted Leave. Remain won among under 45s, Leave among over-45s. Reflecting the fact that, for most people, Brexit was a proxy for a world view, on almost every conceivable social and cultural issue there is a vast difference in outlook between older people and younger people. This is fundamentally important because most people don't fundamentally change their core values as they get older. It is an established pattern that voters tend to become more Conservative on economic issues as they age – though that tendency has weakened alongside the decline in marriage and the rate of home ownership among the 18 to 35s. But someone in their twenties who believes, for example, that multiculturalism is a force for good in the world – which is one of the starkest values divides between older and younger people, and between Remainers and Leavers – is very unlikely to change their mind about that as they get older. The Tory identification with Brexit and with the 'closed' values that are so closely associated with it are defining positions. Millions of younger voters will never forget or forgive.

The Conservative Party, in its post-2016 incarnation, is doubling down on a shrinking demographic. To put it crudely, the number of voters with 'closed' values is diminishing one funeral at a time; very few younger people see – or will ever see – the world in the way that hardcore Brexiteers do. This is what lies behind the comically dreadful poll ratings for the Conservative Party among younger voters. It leaves them heavily dependent electorally on an increasingly elderly cohort of 'closed' values voters.

Brexit denial

Brexit leaves the Tories with a further poisonous legacy. In the same way that success in the US Republican Party now requires a refusal to acknowledge that Trump lost the 2020 presidential election, viability in today's Conservative Party requires the pretence that Brexit is turning out to be a success. A 'Big Lie' rests at the heart of both parties. It is self-evident to most voters that the promised benefits of Brexit have not materialised. It turned out to be much harder and more complicated than the Leave campaigners all insisted. We could not have our cake and eat it, after all. The cost to the economy, the disruption to the lives of ordinary people and the damage done to UK business are all palpable.

YouGov has been regularly asking, since shortly after the referendum, whether Brexit was the right decision or the wrong decision. They have polled this question more than 160 times over the last five years. In that time, only once, in March 2021, has there been a plurality for Brexit being the right decision. Over the last two years the margin by which voters think Brexit was the wrong decision has continued to widen. In the most recent poll,[16] that margin stands at 23 per cent, with less than a third of voters still thinking that Brexit was the right decision. According to YouGov's data, only seven in ten of those who voted to leave the EU now think this was the right decision. The only age group among whom more think Brexit was right than wrong is the over-65s. As the political analyst and pollster Peter Kellner has concluded, 'given how slowly public opinion has changed, this looks like a verdict that is as settled as anything ever is in politics. Britain is no longer a pro-Brexit country.' The demographics of the issue mean that the balance of view will continue to shift further against Brexit over time.

The Conservative Party's refusal – or inability – to acknowledge the reality of Brexit, preferring instead to bury its head in the sand, will become an ever-bigger barrier with voters. It also causes immense continuing damage to the country.

The Tory government is surely right to make economic growth one of its key priorities; it is understandable that growth and the NHS are the two issues featuring on both Rishi Sunak's list of five priorities and Keir Starmer's list of five missions. But if stronger economic growth is indeed a high priority for the country one of the most obvious policies that follows must be to increase the volume of trade between the UK and the European Union. The Office for Budget Responsibility estimates that UK–EU trade in goods is down around eighteen per cent and trade in services is down around 30 per cent since Brexit. It is difficult entirely to disentangle the Brexit effect from the impact of Covid and of the Russian invasion of Ukraine, but all evidence is that leaving the EU has had a significant negative impact on trade. The OBR expects the impact of Brexit alone – regardless of any other factors – to reduce the UK's long-run productivity by four per cent, exports and imports by fifteen per cent and GDP by four per cent. Economic modelling is, self-evidently, not an exact science. But these are the best estimates of the UK government's official forecasting body. And yet the Conservative government's official stance is to deny these facts, because to accept them would force them to acknowledge they got Brexit wrong, something that neither most leading Tories, nor most of the 'closed' values voters on whom they have staked their electoral future, are yet ready to face up to.

Conclusion

Two years before the Brexit referendum, the Conservative member for Clacton quit the Conservative Party, joined UKIP and forced a by-election in his constituency, which he decisively won. At the subsequent general election in 2015, Clacton was the only place in the UK to elect a UKIP member of parliament. In the Brexit referendum, Clacton tied for the highest Leave vote of any constituency (73%). In terms of its aggregate demographics, Clacton is one of the poorest, oldest, least well educated, least healthy and most non-diverse places in the UK.

During the 2014 by-election, the journalist and former Tory MP Matthew Parris went to Clacton to write about the campaign. The column he subsequently wrote[17] was harsh in its depiction of the reality of life there, but his warning about the trajectory of the Conservative Party was acute and prescient. Many right-wing Tories, he noted, wanted to invest the party's political future in 'the disappointed, the angry, the nostalgic and the fearful', of whom there were many in Clacton. This, he observed, would not be a crazy strategy, 'because the market in pessimism is easy to capture, and easier to hold on to than the market in optimism'. There were, he said, many people in places like Clacton who might be attracted to the Tories 'by a noisy display of hostility towards immigration-and-Europe, political correctness and health-and-safety: hostility to a Britain that has forgotten the joys of Ken Dodd, meat pies, smoking in pubs and the Bee Gees'.

The question flowing from this, Matthew Parris rightly concluded, was not whether this may be a politically profitable place for the Conservatives to be in the short run and in some places, but whether it is where they should *want* to be, or '*need* to be if they're to gather momentum in this century, rather than slowly lose it?' By tacking towards 'closed' values and allowing itself to become singly defined by Brexit, the

Conservative Party has, in effect, bet on the past against the future; on the myth of a restored 'closed' past over the challenging opportunity of an 'open' reality.

In his brilliant speech to the Labour Party conference in 1985 – when he turned on the extremists who had tried to take over the party – Neil Kinnock used a quotation from Aneurin Bevan's 1952 book *In Place of Fear*. It aptly applies to the Conservative Party today: 'Be on guard against the old words, for the words persist when the reality that lay behind them has changed. It is inherent in our intellectual activity that we seek to imprison reality in our description of it. Soon, long before we are aware of it, it is we who become the prisoners of the description. From that point on, our ideas degenerate into a kind of folklore which we pass around to each other, fondly thinking that we are still talking of the reality around us. We become symbol worshippers.' That is today's Conservative Party: symbol worshippers.

The three-time Pulitzer prize-winning *New York Times* columnist Thomas Friedman spent some time in Britain in 2019 and captured his reflections in an article memorably headed 'The United Kingdom has gone mad.'[18]

He put his observations about the UK in the context that it is the responsibility of leaders to be honest about the realities of the world we live in – both with themselves and with the people whose lives are affected by their decisions. That reality, as Friedman described it, is:

> a world that is becoming so *interconnected* – thanks to digitisation, the internet, broadband, mobile devices, the cloud and soon-to-be 5G wireless transmissions – that we are becoming *interdependent* to an unprecedented degree. In this world, growth increasingly depends on the ability of yourself, your community, your town, your factory, your school and your country to be connected to more and more of the *flows* of knowledge and investment.

The world is, in other words (and whether we like it or not), 'open'.

'And yet,' as Thomas Friedman ruefully concluded, 'Britain is now ruled by a party that wants to disconnect from a connected world.'

This frame – connected/disconnected – used to be at the heart of the Conservative Party's thinking. David Cameron, the last Conservative leader to embrace 'open' values rather than pander to 'closed' ones, often spoke about the UK being 'in a global race'. In an open, globalised world, countries thrive by having clear long-term strategies to improve education and modernise skills, to grasp the revolutionary momentum of new technology, by being ambitious, entrepreneurial and aspirational – not by the comfort blanket of a largely mythological idea of British exceptionalism, which is so often the default of Tories today.

It is not a coincidence that many of the most Brexity places in Britain are – like Clacton – around the edges: decaying seaside towns. They are physically as well as politically and psychologically disconnected from the country's economic hubs; unplugged from the literal and metaphorical networks that power a modern society; cut off from the flows of knowledge and investment.

The voters of Clacton came decisively to the collective conclusion that Brexit would improve the economic and social outlook of their community. They took refuge in 'closed' values. This is what led Matthew Parris to conclude 'I am not arguing that we should be careless of the needs of struggling people and places like Clacton. But I am arguing – if I am honest – that we should be careless of their opinions.' They were wrong about Brexit, which will make their lives harder, their prospects bleaker and their futures poorer.

The question that those who believe in 'open' values must, therefore, address is this: if Brexit isn't the solution for places like Clacton, what is? Part of the answer lies in connectedness

– better transport links and broadband connectivity. If Clacton had a high-speed rail link into London, it would be rejuvenated almost overnight. Education and skills are another important part. These are illustrative points, not worked-through solutions and they barely scratch the surface. But it is by fixing these underlying issues, which are real, that we will stand a chance of making Britain less polarised, reconnecting the UK with Europe and the wider world and reconnecting the likes of Clacton with the engine of the UK, showing that with 'open' values the whole of Britain can prosper.

2

Populism's Price

Rory Stewart

In May 2019, Boris Johnson dismissed the idea that he would prorogue parliament. In August 2019, he prorogued parliament, and assured the Queen that his action had nothing to do with Brexit. On 24 September, the Supreme Court ruled that Boris Johnson's prorogation was an unlawful attempt to prevent parliament voting on Brexit. Parliament reassembled. A jetlagged Boris Johnson entered the parliamentary chamber from behind the Speaker's Chair, having just landed from New York.

It is likely that previous British prime ministers would have responded to the Supreme Court with a rueful, if slightly pompous, tribute to the importance of the constitution, parliamentary sovereignty and the rule of law. But this was Boris Johnson. Johnson attacked the ruling, pouring scorn on a 'paralysed parliament' and MPs who have 'done all they can to abandon [their] promises and to overturn the democratic vote'. He called parliament's bill to block no-deal 'the surrender Act'. His anarchically exuberant body language was now harnessed to a more aggressive language. Falstaff was becoming Trump. 'Out of sheer political selfishness and political cowardice', he roared, 'Opposition Members are unwilling to move aside and give the people a say. We will not betray the people who sent us here; we will not . . .'

As he concluded, the whips behind the Speaker's chair lifted their hands like conductors, and the choir of Conservative loyalists reached a roaring crescendo. Boris Johnson, who once had a reputation as a genial, elusive clown, with imprecise and unpinnable ideas, had shape-shifted into a tribune of the people insisting on clarity and resolution. He had become a populist.

The break from the liberal centre right

At first sight Boris Johnson was doing nothing new or particularly shocking. Many politicians in every party portray themselves as standing for people against an out-of-touch elite, and seek to create clear blue water between themselves and their opponents. All make promises, some of which were not delivered. And his support base was familiar. Johnson enlisted much of the Conservative Party, most Conservative MPs and many Cameron loyalists, including Liz Truss and Matt Hancock, who were happy to serve in his cabinet. He was not a fascist: he did not celebrate racism, glorify violence, or assert a radical 'leadership principle'. He cloaked his performance in far more jokes, charm, linguistic exuberance and classical references than did Donald Trump. Nevertheless, Boris Johnson represented a fundamental break from the liberal centre right tradition of the Conservative Party towards populism.

Johnson's new populism was embedded in his attitudes to pluralism, the constitution, truth, and polarisation. When he spoke in the House of Commons, he no longer claimed to speak only for the Conservative Party or Conservative voters, but instead for the 'people' as a whole. He characterised his opponents – including the sixteen million people who had voted for Remain – not as half the population of the United

Kingdom but instead as part of an alien and dishonest elite, subverting the will of 'the people'. He rejected the notion of a loyal opposition, and he caricatured any attempt at compromise, in the form of a softer Brexit, as treachery and sham. Having previously claimed that he was leaving the European Union in order to assert the sovereignty of parliament and the British courts, he treated parliament and the courts with contempt. His priority was power and, when the constitution ceased to facilitate that, he condemned it.

Johnson's inconsistency and dishonesty were flamboyantly public. He insisted that he alone could take Britain out of the EU by 31 October, knowing it was impossible. He insisted that he could avoid a border in the Irish sea, when he could not. He insisted in August that the prorogation had nothing to do with Brexit, and then claimed the opposite when it suited him two weeks later. But he made these contradictory and implausible claims not to convince, so much as to muddy waters, unsettle critics, sow doubt and buy time in the political debate.

And, having seized powers through this lurching mendacity, he sought not to heal but to polarise an already bitterly divided population. Boris Johnson's speech in parliament and his subsequent interventions in the 2019 election were not intended to reconcile these groups, persuade, find compromise, or to balance the demands of the majority against the interests of minority. Instead, he exacerbated divisions. In response to a request for compromise and moderation, he insisted 'There was a very clear dividing line, and I know which side I am on . . .' He was 'sticking up for' 'the will of the people'.

His predecessors Theresa May and David Cameron were in these respects not simply, by contrast, leaders of the liberal centre right, they were, in retrospect, the last representatives of the pre-populist global order. The first two decades of their political careers, from 1988 (the year that Cameron entered Conservative central office and May became a chairperson on her local Conservative council) was a period of triumph for liberal democracy. Across the world, Communism collapsed, the number of democracies in the world doubled, global median income rose by 43 per cent, global inequality fell substantially. Every year, the world became less violent and more prosperous: there was a dramatic decline in all forms of warfare and the number of refugees. This was the background against which Francis Fukuyama declared that the world had reached 'the end-point of mankind's ideological evolution and the universalisation of Western liberal democracy as the final form of human government'.

David Cameron was consciously centrist. He made no secret of his admiration for Tony Blair or his contempt for the 'fruitcakes', 'loonies' and 'closet racists' seeking to leave the European Union and he sought to win elections in the centre ground. There were, of course, problems with his embrace of the global consensus: he did not challenge the global financial system before 2008, or vote against the war in Iraq, or question warm relations with China. Compared to Johnson, however, Cameron was diligent, comparatively truthful, and respectful of parliament, courts and the opposition. And he was committed to a pluralist, socially liberal conservatism. He transformed the diversity of the Conservative parliamentary party – putting eight MPs from ethnic minority backgrounds on track to be secretaries of state, when there had been none under previous government. He brought through the first legislation for gay marriage. He doubled the amount that Britain spent on international development assistance. He was happy to combine with other political parties in his campaign against Scottish independence. He attempted to clear petty corruption out of parliament after the expenses scandal. He was respectful towards the permanent civil service. He did not attempt to stir identity politics or culture wars. He was in rhetoric and substance a pluralist.

His successor, Theresa May, inherited a profound realignment in British politics, triggered by Brexit, and her statement of her Conservative philosophy in the new manifesto seemed to owe more to Edmund Burke and the Tory vision of 'One Nation' than to the Davos global order. But her form of liberal conservatism continued to focus on healing rather than polarisation:

> We abhor social division, injustice, unfairness and inequality. We see rigid dogma and ideology not just as needless but dangerous. True conservatism means a commitment to country and community; a belief not just in society but in the good that government can do; a respect for the local and national institutions that bind us together . . . We respect the fact that society is a contract between the generations: a partnership between those who are living, those who have lived before us, and those who are yet to be born.

Even after losing her majority in the 2017 election, May remained respectful towards court rulings and international agreements. She sought to negotiate and pass a softer compromise Brexit modelled on a customs union, in part because she thought it was necessary to respect the Catholic minority and preserve peace in Northern Ireland. And she was ultimately willing to work with Labour votes to bring her deal through. Populist temptations in the Conservative Party, in other words, continued to be moderated with elements of liberalism, democratic pluralism, traditional morality and a range of uncodified checks and balances.

Nevertheless, disturbing weaknesses were already apparent. Despite May's evident seriousness, the culture of British politics in a post-ideological age seemed often to be focused more on winning elections than governing well. Marketing, social media, polling, 24-hour media coverage and campaign financing often seemed more important than the integrity and moral authority of politicians. Ministers promoted fast under David Cameron – Liz Truss and Priti Patel for example – were not always selected on the basis of their capacity for imaginative sympathy, or ability to grasp rapidly changing, contradictory information. As an MP in 2010, I found a culture that was often antithetical to sustained and serious thought. Inside parliament, whips and party managers focused their energy on games and briefing against the opposition, reducing political debate to propaganda, and turning dignified MPs into humiliated puppets. Able MPs were regularly overlooked, and some of the most arrogant, unreliable, and poorly informed, promoted. I was no exception.

As a minister I was frequently placed in roles for which I had no expertise. When I took responsibility for air pollution, which was killing tens of thousands, or a Malawi school system in which 85 per cent of girls graduated unable to read or write – I found a system that responded with abstractions, and evasions. As soon as I developed an understanding of my brief, I was reshuffled. And I was ultimately promoted to the cabinet because of loyalty, not performance. Even the finest civil service could not compensate for such ineptitude. And our civil service was not perfect. Meanwhile, living a political life often seemed to be enervating the qualities required to act responsibly in the Cabinet Room.

Little wonder that we so manifestly failed to meet the challenges of governance: that so much in Britain remained shameful (prisons), embarrassing (Malawi), tragic (Iraq and Afghanistan), or even horrifying. Little wonder that we did not resolve the fundamental problems of an ageing population, dependent on cheap energy, food and goods from hostile or unfriendly countries. And had no answers on what we would we do if drought destroyed crops from Somalia to California, or our prices soared.

In some ways, the politics prevalent from 2005 already anticipated many of the stylistic features of populism. While critical thinking required humility, the new politics increasingly demanded absolute confidence: in place of reality, it

offered untethered hope; instead of accuracy, vagueness. While
critical thinking required scepticism, open-mindedness and an
instinct for complexity; this politics already often demanded
loyalty, partisanship and slogans. The public were right to
doubt the seriousness, respect, critical thought and concern
for detail in their governing class.

This coarsening of standards of governing and parliamentary life combined with a global collapse in the credibility
of liberal democracies and markets. In 2005, the number of
democracies ceased, for the first time, to grow, the Chinese
economy became larger than the UK economy, and US global
leadership was fatally wounded by the developing humiliations
in Iraq and Afghanistan. 2008 brought the financial crisis,
alienation from the global system and political leadership, and
a near permanent blow to British productivity. In 2011, the
Arab Spring demonstrated how Twitter and Facebook could
spread political unrest instantly across very different national
frontiers. In 2012, Putin became President of Russia again, and
Xi Jinping became Premier of China. In 2003, just twelve per
cent of the British public felt that the quality of life for youth
would be lower than that of their parents. In 2011, one third
felt that youth would have a worse standard of life. By 2016, a
majority of the public now thought that quality of life for youth
would be lower than that of their parents.

The populist turn

The age of populism began in 2014: the year in which Putin
invaded Crimea, Isis declared a caliphate, and Narendra Modi
was elected in India. In quick succession, the election of the
Law and Justice Party in Poland in 2015, of Donald Trump
in the United States in 2016, and Jair Bolsonaro in Brazil in
2018, brought provocative, anarchic, charismatic leaders to
four continents – all of whom gained traction, by spitting

out half-invented facts, polarising the public, and presenting themselves as tribunes of the people in revolt against an unrepresentative elite. The retreat of the US and its allies from 'policing' the liberal world order coincided with an explosion of violence. Every year now coincided with a decline in global human rights, and the number of democracies. Between 2005 and 2016 the number of refugees and internally displaced persons (IDPs) doubled, and the number of battlefield deaths increased tenfold. The number of civilian deaths in violent conflicts doubled between 2010 and 2016.

This was the global context of the Brexit referendum in 2016. And it immediately revealed the fragility of assumptions about Britain as a moderate consensual society. Groups who wanted either hard Brexit, or no Brexit at all, split into one of the most polarised political environments since the English civil war. According to opinion polls, less than half of the voters on different sides of Brexit were prepared even to speak to their opponents; less than a quarter would contemplate their child marrying a child from a family on the other side. Both embraced almost indistinguishable populist tropes. The hard Brexiteers claimed that they were the 'real people'; that their opponents had been duped by bankers and politicians, who had conspired with the Treasury and the European super-state to produce dishonest doomsday predictions about mass unemployment and a third world war and they promised a Britain that need make no compromise, pay no money, accept no rules from Europe, on its path to greatness and prosperity.

This narrative had an exact shadow. In the hard Remain fairytale, the 'real people' were the 48 per cent who had voted Remain. Those who voted for Brexit were an unrepresentative coalition of the racist and the uneducated; the marginalised and the elderly, who were ignorant of the true facts, and who had been duped by financiers and politicians who had stolen the referendum through lies on the side of buses, with the sinister abuse of big data, and with Russian money. The referendum was itself purely advisory. It needed to be rejected, or at least run again. And then the wise saviours could simply restore the status quo. Britain would return to the European Union in exactly the same position it had been before.

Both factions in the country used almost identical language. Both claimed to speak for the 'real people'. Both characterised their enemy as a corrupt elite. Both supported democratic votes, elections, parliament or the courts, but only when these institutions produced the results they wanted. And, when they didn't, both sides were willing to abuse parliamentary procedure and bypass public votes in the name of a higher cause. Both claimed to be the victims of a Twitter war. Both claimed that the media were biased against them. The Brexit leader, Nigel Farage, referred to the BBC as the 'Brussels broadcasting corporation', the leading Remainer, Andrew Adonis, called it the 'Brexit broadcasting corporation'. Both sides saw advocates for Theresa May's deal as extreme partisans, simply cloaking their agenda in reasonable sounding language, although they disagreed fundamentally on whether May was a Brexiteer or a Remainer.

Boris Johnson was the heir to all of this: the financial crisis, public despair, the collapse of the liberal 'global order', social media's ability to create instant, unstable, coalitions of dissent, and the polarisation of Brexit. Like his counterpart in Jeremy Corbyn, he appealed to a deep nostalgia for an imagined lost Britain, and rejected all traditional consensus as an establishment conspiracy. Both competed to deny the complexity of society and economy. Both misrepresented what Britain shared, and what it could realistically be.

Nevertheless, the brutality, cynicism and shamelessness of Boris Johnson's response to this crisis was startling and unprecedented. Within three months of taking office, Boris Johnson had illegally prorogued parliament, and attacked the Supreme Court for over-ruling him, and destroyed the one-nation tradition of the Conservative Party. He had expelled the leading champions of the liberal centre right from the Conservative

Party and parliament, dismissed two-thirds of Theresa May's cabinet ministers and replaced them with a team of loyalists. He appointed as ministers people who had been fired by David Cameron or Theresa May for business malpractice, inappropriate relations with foreign powers, breaches of national security, or sexual misconduct.

His first ethics adviser resigned because Johnson refused to sanction a cabinet minister for bullying. His second resigned because of the Prime Minister's dishonesty around financial donations. Johnson responded by refusing to appoint a third ethics adviser. He took and did not publicly declare an £800,000 loan and then appointed the man who had facilitated that loan as the Chairman of the BBC. He lied repeatedly to the House of Commons and changed the sections of the ministerial code so that it was no longer necessary for lying ministers to resign. Through all this, many Conservative MPs continued to support him, serve in his cabinet, and defend his malfeasances and scandals in public. He distracted from scandals with campaigns and culture wars, which were designed to attract more right-wing, socially conservative Brexit voters and MPs in northern England. And, to remain in power, he danced across the spinning tops of an ever more factionalised and ideological Conservative Party: flattering libertarians and social conservatives, cheap fuel advocates and environmentalists, fox-hunters and tech-enthusiasts.

The increasing, accelerating turbulence of Boris Johnson's rule shattered his party, undermined the economy and discredited the state. Ultimately his contradictions became too evident, and MPs were no longer prepared to forgive his reckless, immoral, embarrassing dishonesty as simply anarchic exuberance. He left behind an increasingly unmanageable party, which voted for Liz Truss, whose promises were ever simpler and bolder and who had even less patience for prudence and intractable realities. Yet, it was only five years since the Conservative Party had prided itself on being a broad

coalition, in which cabinet ministers mostly kept their jobs
under new prime ministers, votes were in the centre ground,
and Britain's brand was moderation and prudence – the
irritating but 'sensible' voice in Europe and international
affairs.

The way back

How should the liberal centre right respond to populism? One
possible answer is that they can't, because the deterioration of
the liberal global order had permanently discredited the hopes
for a liberal centre. Public opinion had been, in the time of
Blair and Cameron, a bell curve, with all the votes in the centre
ground. Now the bell shape had collapsed, like an unstable
souffle, into a U-shape, leaving voters only on the extremes.

But there are many signs across the world that the shift to
populism is not permanent. In 2020, Joe Biden, the epitome of
the old Democratic establishment, defeated Donald Trump,
and survived the 6 January insurrection. In 2022, populists
were defeated in Slovenia, the Czech Republic and the US
Senate. In Australia the teal independents – epitomes of the
liberal centre right – won a series of significant victories.
Bolsonaro lost in Brazil and Macron defeated Marine Le Pen in
France. And, despite all the ambiguity and fragility of Britain's
unwritten constitution, the British parliamentary system was
able to dismiss Boris Johnson and then his successor Liz Truss,
and replace them with the more restrained and thoughtful
figure of Rishi Sunak.

Populism is, therefore, not inescapable. But it is peculiarly
well suited to an age of disillusionment, authoritarianism and
social media. The devil has the best tunes. Fighting it is far
more difficult than it felt in the heyday of Anglo-American
liberal democracy. And it needs to be challenged from many
angles simultaneously. We cannot shy away from a renewed

emphasis on truth, consistency and integrity in politics, on Cicero's pompous but important observation that politicians are not born for themselves alone, but for their country, and on the importance of refusing to collaborate with populist power. Faced with serving in Boris Johnson's cabinet and defending his scandals and malfeasance in the television studios, more MPs should have considered the possibility of resignation and refusing power. When they did, in large numbers, they brought him down.

The second response must be to attempt – in the absence of saints – to design institutions that can protect us better from irresponsible demagogues. That was part, of course, of the project of the American founders. And it could be adapted for a contemporary British context. If we are entering an age of prime ministers unashamed to do things previously considered unthinkable, then we need to tighten our constitution. If our parties – embedded in our state by a first-past-the-post electoral system – are becoming ever narrower and less representative, we should introduce a proportional electoral system to allow new smaller parties, with different cultures, to enter parliament, and broaden the ideologies on offer through coalition governments. If wealthy donors and trade unions create grotesque conflicts of interest we could consider state funding of parties. To connect politics more tightly to local issues we should give elected mayors more revenue raising powers and responsibilities. To generate new compromises on difficult issues, and escape the trap of party politics, we should use citizen assemblies.

But the most immediate task is to revive the appeal of the liberal centre right. This revival must be rooted in a better approach to governing: demonstrating thoughtfulness, diligence, command of detail, efficiency and results and, by doing so, exposing the vacuous abstractions of the populists. Rishi Sunak did much of this in the Windsor negotiations on Northern Ireland. But, as Aristotle observed this, is not enough: to succeed the logos – or reason – of politics must be also combined with pathos – emotion, and ethos – character.

The lack of resonant emotional arguments is an enduring weakness of the liberal centre right, perhaps because its decades of dominance made such arguments seem unnecessary, and the moderate character of liberal centre right politicians made them uneasy with grander sentiments. From the late Blair era, centrist policies seemed too often surrendered to think tanks recommending better use of technology, or more attention to Finnish classrooms. Often the only 'value' emphasised was value for money. This was apparent in the Labour and Conservative political campaigns, which often lacked authenticity, and boldness – content to echo opinion polls but shying away from a bold diagnosis of the nation's present and future. This provided an opportunity for the populists to satirise the centre, to monopolise humour, outrage and the more confident punchy language of patriotism and liberty, and to use emotional rhetoric as a convenient cloaking for their hollowness.

But the ability to inspire a crowd should not be confined to demagogues. A sense of humour need not be a monopoly of charlatans. After all, Harold Macmillan, the quintessential intellectual leader of the conservative liberal centre, was never shy of showmanship or even a streak of vulgarity. And there is no reason why leaders of the liberal centre should not aim to emulate the charisma of Bill Clinton or the rhetorical and conceptual ambition of Barack Obama.

The most striking gap in the liberal central right, however, lies in what Aristotle calls ethos – or moral character. Again, because its leaders were the architects and administrators of the existing order, they ceased to acknowledge how much was genuinely pathetic and shameful about British government. They could seem almost indifferent to rickety public services, an underwhelming economy, inept foreign and defence policy, grotesquely distorted housing markets, a grotesque criminal justice system, and shocking treatment of the elderly. There was a surreal gap between the pretensions of the government and the reality that surrounded citizens. And the governing class failed to demonstrate, and often to feel, empathy, shame and moral outrage. Little wonder that many of the disciples of Cameron and Osborne seemed so comfortable serving and defending Boris Johnson.

In order to revive, the liberal centre right has to be broader and more generous in terms of the issues that it embraces, the populations it addresses, and the confidence of its moral stance. It cannot remain a purely pragmatic project, stripped of moral content. It cannot be a purely technocratic project, insisting snobbishly on a single truth. It should not be a narrowing project – which seeks simply to belittle the intuitions, the understanding or the motivations of people who favoured Boris Johnson, or even Jeremy Corbyn. It cannot run away from conversations about its own failures on immigration, globalisation, stagnant incomes, crime, or identity. It must embrace what is radical and uncomfortable about difficult truths and find, through a greater commitment to empathy and reality, a connective power and a maturity, which populism cannot match.

In other words, the liberal centre right needs to be based in what the pre-Socratic philosopher Heraclitus called 'a harmony like that of the bow or the lyre'. The killing power of the bow or the beautiful sound of the lyre derive from strings held under tension. In the words of the psychiatrist Iain McGilchrist, 'the stable complex whole is balanced and efficient not despite, but *because of* a pulling in opposite directions'.

Which is to say, when faced with an electorate that sometimes feels as though all the votes are gathered at two opposite ends of a stick, the liberal centre right should not be simply the midpoint of the stick, whose only merit is being as far away as possible from each extreme. It should seek instead to connect both ends with a string to make a bow. And in this case, the centre should not be on the stick at all, but at the midpoint of the string, the point of greatest potential energy – which comes, not from excluding the extremes, but instead from harnessing what is positive in the wisdom, the passion and the moral insights within these opposing forces. And not only their competing claims for justice and liberty.

3

Restoring the Rule of Law
Dominic Grieve

Who needs the rule of law? That this question has to be asked in a book dedicated to centre right conservatism is in itself remarkable. As David Gauke has explained in his introduction, external perceptions of the United Kingdom have historically been of a nation of strong institutions with the rule of law at its heart, underpinning their functioning.

While not confined to the centre right, respect for the rule of law has also long had a distinctively conservative edge to it. Anger at social injustice has often been a hallmark of the left in politics. With it has come a temptation to justify lawbreaking, and even violence, as legitimate means of achieving social or political change, whether at home or abroad. The same can be seen on the populist right, where anger often drives demands. In contrast, traditional Conservatives have been much warier of the consequences of disregard for the law. We have taken a distinctive and at times rather romantic view of our nation's history, that has centred on events from Magna Carta in 1215 to Habeas Corpus in 1672 and the Bill of Rights of 1689. All of these were landmarks in the prevention of the abuse of royal/ state power. They required the law to be observed by all, protected liberties and helped create government only with the consent of parliament, laying the foundations of our modern parliamentary democracy and, with it, the ability to make political change without violence. We have also celebrated the unique flexibility of the common law system of justice we enjoy in England, Wales and Northern Ireland and its continuous development over the centuries.

An emphasis on the rule of law usually resonates with conservative economic principles. It underpins growth by providing fair and legitimate routes for dispute resolution, reducing corruption and creating certainty that contracts will be enforced and international trade and investment can flourish. It is the essence of 'quiet government' that successive Conservative prime ministers have traditionally sought to deliver. Even when carrying out difficult reforms, Margaret Thatcher placed it at the heart of her administration, stating that 'the institution of democracy alone is not enough. Liberty can only flourish under a rule of law.'[1] Trained as a lawyer, she was a stickler for its observance.

The rule of law has also been central to our approach to international relations. Notwithstanding pride in our sovereignty, the UK has, even at the height of its imperial power, sought to make the world a safer and more predictable place by participating in the creation of international agreements governing the behaviour of states. When I was Attorney General, I once enquired as to how many treaties we were adherent. The Foreign Office was unwilling to go back beyond 1834, but, since then, they had records of around 13,200 and the figure is now over 14,000, making us probably the greatest treaty-making power in world history. Many hundreds of treaties contain binding dispute resolution mechanisms in the event of disagreements over interpretation. Since the end of the Second World War these treaties, be they the ECHR, the UN Convention on the Rights of the Child or the treaty creating the International Criminal Court, have dealt not just with inter-state relations, but with standards of behaviour of a state towards those over whom it exercises power. In each case, by signing up we have made it a duty on the UK through its ministers and public officials to try to uphold their terms.

But this historic picture of support for the principles of the rule of law is now being undermined by increasingly strident arguments from within the Conservative Party that the framework of laws we have are acting as a fetter on the views of the electorate, parliamentary sovereignty and executive discretion. Ministers today may denounce Russia for not adhering to the 'international rules-based system' by attacking Ukraine. But they have been willing to threaten to do it themselves over the NI Protocol, notwithstanding that they themselves signed up to it only three years ago.

In this chapter, I want to explore briefly how this phenomenon has come about, its consequences and what those of us on the liberal centre right need to do about it.

Human rights

A good starting point is the European Convention on Human Rights (ECHR) and its incorporation into our own law through the Human Rights Act (HRA). The Convention was created, in significant part, by British lawyers in response to the horrors of the Second World War and in order to try to prevent any resurgence in Europe of the gross violations of rights that had characterised Nazism and Fascism and were then continuing in those parts of our continent under the domination of Communism. At the time, the Convention, when signed up to by the UK, was seen, with the exception of Article 8 on privacy and the right to a family life, as a classic exposition of the 'liberties' that the British claimed as a shared and exceptional inheritance. After all, it protects the right to life, liberty and security, a fair trial, freedom of conscience, religion and expression, marriage, and prohibits torture and retroactive criminalisation. It was later amended to protect the right to free and fair elections. There were some concerns among both Labour and Conservative MPs, however, about translating those broad principles, in which we took pride, into an international legal obligation that might as a last resort be interpreted by an international tribunal. But these were overcome by a sense of responsibility for promoting these principles internationally. So we signed and ratified it, agreed to observe it, saw the Court set up in 1959 and, in 1966, decided with Conservative Party support to allow individuals rather than just states to bring claims under it.

We have certainly been successful in our broad aim. The promotion of human rights is seen as a major success brought about by UK soft power and influence. In the ensuing seventy years, the ECHR and the Strasbourg-based European Court of Human Rights (ECtHR), which interprets its terms, have been instrumental in transforming standards of human rights in many European countries and provides an important backstop, particularly in countries that have more recently become democracies. Examples range from ending discrimination against children on the grounds of illegitimacy; ending corporal punishment in schools; prohibiting interrogation techniques that constitute inhuman/degrading treatment; requiring access to a lawyer for a detained suspect at the earliest opportunity, and requiring civil partnerships to be open to same-sex couples.

It has sometimes been a little challenging that a number of cases has also concerned matters in which the UK has been found wanting. But, until the mid 1990s, Conservatives accepted that the benefits of adherence and of those adverse judgments, being then applied elsewhere, outweighed any irritation and I can't think of one judgment today that any government would seek to reverse. But there was then a change in attitude. Michael Howard, as Home Secretary, complained of the Strasbourg Court decision in Chahal vs. UK,[2] which prevented the deportation of a suspected Sikh terrorist to India on the grounds of there being a risk of torture, despite the assurances he had secured. He considered that this decision should have been left to the Executive. This attitude then coloured the Conservative approach to incorporation of the ECHR into our law through the Human Rights Act. Notwithstanding the careful way it was drafted to preserve all the principles of parliamentary sovereignty, we refused to support it.

Sections of the Conservative Right have been grumbling ever since. It was David Cameron who insisted, when Leader and then Prime Minister, on trying to replace the HRA with a 'British Bill of Rights' that would somehow enable us to 'clarify' Convention rights, particularly those prohibiting torture and giving a right to a family life, so as to prevent their abuse in deportation cases by changing the tests to be applied. The Convention rights were to be confined to *'cases that involve criminal law and the liberty of the individual and other serious matters'*,[3] with parliament setting a threshold below which no Convention right would be enforceable. We would legislate to no longer require our courts to take account of decisions on similar cases at the ECtHR. The UK was effectively to demand a special status, where judgments from the ECtHR were merely advisory or else, if that didn't happen, leave the Convention, so thereafter all the Executive's irritations would be removed.

At the time, it was pointed out that the proposals contained factual errors and defects in argument. It was widely criticised and indeed ridiculed. But it still featured in the 2015 Conservative Party Manifesto, but was not pursued because David Cameron ceased to be Prime Minister and Theresa May was wise enough to see it was unworkable. But it was, however, revived by Boris Johnson. In response, the then Justice Secretary Robert Buckland set up an independent commission under Sir Peter Gross to do an analysis of options as to how the HRA might be changed compatibly with staying in the

ECHR, and he came up, not surprisingly, with some sensible but modest ideas, because very little change was either possible or desirable. Yet Dominic Raab later returned to most of the 2015 version. As has been pointed out by a retired Supreme Court Judge, Lord Mance, the Bill, if enacted, solves nothing. It is just a recipe for further conflicts between the Executive and both domestic and international courts.[4] More cases will end up in the Strasbourg ECtHR and there are likely to be more findings against the UK.

The irony of all this is that it also undoes a decade of the UK influencing the ECtHR in ways that Conservatives should approve. There were legitimate criticisms then that the ECtHR had become a micro manager of rights, failing to give both domestic courts and parliaments enough leeway in how human rights principles are applied. There was widespread irritation with the ECtHR's judgment that a blanket prohibition in the UK on prisoners voting in elections was in breach of the Convention. But, in the years in between, much has changed. Led by Kenneth Clarke, when Justice Secretary, traditional diplomacy delivered the Brighton Declaration, which gently reformed both the ECtHR's processes in sifting cases and its attitude to different interpretations of the Convention rights. An excellent judicial dialogue has been developed between our own Supreme Court and the ECtHR that has done much to influence the latter's approach. The stand off with the Court over prisoner voting was resolved by David Lidington when Lord Chancellor, without any need at all for legislation or domestic political fallout. In 2022, as a snapshot, 240 UK applications were allocated to judges of the ECtHR but there were only two findings against the UK.[5] We attract the fewest complaints to the Court per capita of any adherent state.

Yet, with the latest threats from Suella Braverman, speaking as Home Secretary, that we will pull out of the ECHR altogether if her current plans to deal with asylum seekers coming to our country illegally are in any way obstructed, we risk losing our reputation and the goodwill that goes with it. Not only will it make it harder to persuade any court, domestic or international, that we will have legislated compatibly with the ECHR in any changes we make to our immigration, but the threat to leave looks like angry and reckless Trump-style politics. Shared adherence to the ECHR is a key component in our Trade and Co-operation agreement with the EU, and leaving the ECHR will make parts of it unworkable, including security co-operation and data sharing, which is essential not just for security but also for business. The existence in Northern Ireland of the rights under the Convention and adherence to it by the UK also underpins the Belfast/Good Friday Agreement. No credible explanation whatever has been provided by a Conservative government as to how dishonouring these obligations would be handled, or what possible benefit might come from doing so that outweighs the practical and reputational costs.

The Brexit effect

It would be pleasant if it could be said that this long-running saga over the ECHR was an isolated eccentricity in the usual Conservative support for the rule of law and an international rules-based system. In the years up to the EU referendum, criticism of the ECHR seemed at times a proxy for criticism of erosions of sovereignty by the EU, even though the two are unrelated. One might have hoped, therefore, that the decision to leave the EU would have had a calming impact on the views of the populist right. But events since suggest that the reverse is the case. Frustrations about Brexit being complicated and not rapidly delivering the benefits expected have fuelled attacks on our judiciary, calls to ignore international law when it suits us and a willingness to ignore constitutional conventions and rules on the basis of political necessity.

The first example came soon after the 2016 referendum with the first Miller case.[6] The question as to whether the Executive had power under the Royal Prerogative to trigger Article 50 to leave the EU, or whether a parliamentary statute was needed, was an important but fairly esoteric point of law. The Supreme Court's conclusion that a statute was needed made no difference to Brexit's progress. But the first instance decision of the judges of the Divisional Court when interpreting the law, without 'fear or favour', as was their duty, was greeted by their vilification as 'enemies of the people' by two national newspapers. The response of the then Lord Chancellor Liz Truss, who had taken a specific oath of office a few weeks earlier to *respect the rule of law, (and) defend the independence of the judiciary*, was to say nothing for twenty-four hours and then come out with a totally equivocal statement about the freedom of the press to criticise judicial decisions – and this only after consultation with the Prime Minister's special advisers. Seeing that her original oath had been insisted on by Conservatives, along with others, when the Constitutional Reform Act was enacted in 2005 because there was concern at the risk of judicial independence being eroded, that equivocation was remarkable, as was her refusal, in breach of her own oath, to act independently in giving her support to the judges in their work.

In September 2019 Boris Johnson, as Prime Minister, decided to bypass the opposition of a majority of MPs in the House of Commons to any 'no deal' Brexit by seeking to prorogue parliament for six critical weeks, so that it could not obstruct his strategy for negotiating with the EU and securing an exit from it at the end of October, with or without a deal. This action, unprecedented in modern times, could not be stopped by parliament as it was an exercise of another prerogative power. It led to the second Miller[7] case in the Supreme Court, when Johnson's actions in advising the Queen to prorogue were held to be unlawful. The unanimous judgment of the Court was entirely in keeping with traditional jurisprudence. The exercise of prerogative powers has been judicially reviewable in our courts since the seventeenth century, as the government had to concede. The argument that prorogation was a matter of high policy and therefore the courts should not interfere in it, as the issue should be left to the political arena, was rejected because the government could provide no reasonable explanation to justify preventing parliament from carrying out its proper constitutional function. One reason for there being no explanation was the fact that the Prime Minister had earlier lied about his motives for proroguing and when he had first taken the decision to do it, so that no affidavit from any official giving reasons for doing it was possible.

Irritating as the outcome doubtless was for Johnson, a traditional right of centre respect for the rule of law and the courts might have been expected to see some lessons being learned from this shameful episode of government misconduct. Instead, the Conservative Party Manifesto of 2019 was in part directed at these new sources of political grievance. It said that the Conservatives would focus on 'the relationship between parliament, government and the courts, the functioning of the Royal Prerogative . . .' It pledged to 'update the HRA and administrative law to ensure there is proper balance between the rights of individuals, our vital national security and effective government'. It went on: 'We will ensure that judicial review is available to protect the rights of the individuals [sic] against an overbearing state, while ensuring that this is not abused to conduct politics by another means and to create endless delays.' There was no hint of recognition then, or since, that the courts in both Miller cases might have been protecting the very rights referred to in the manifesto. The 2019 manifesto seems to mark the development of a novel constitutional principle: that governments enjoying the confidence of a parliamentary majority have a popular mandate to do whatever they like and that any obstruction of this is unacceptable.

We have since seen the consequences of these distortions of reality. There has been a rather piecemeal reform of the Judicial Review but no significant change, probably because of the realisation of how difficult it would be to get through the House of Lords. But, with regard to the nation's security, we have had the Overseas Operations (Service Personnel and Veterans) Act 2021, which was intended to end vexatious claims against UK Armed Forces' personnel. Denounced by a former Chief of the General Staff as contrary to all the principles for which the Armed Forces stand, it had to be extensively amended in parliament to remove glaring incompatibilities with international legal obligations, which the UK claims to support as a global champion of human rights. But the end result is still a two-tier limitation period for legal claims that discriminate in favour of Armed Forces personnel and a presumption against prosecution of personnel for many lesser offences after five years. These provisions are almost certainly incompatible with the HRA and do nothing to create greater legal certainty for anyone.

This cavalier attitude to the rule of law was also apparent with the Internal Market Bill in late 2020. In this first attempt to override the Northern Ireland Protocol, signed as part of an international treaty only a year earlier, the then Secretary of State for Northern Ireland was happy to admit when supporting it that it breached international law in a 'specific and limited way', and the then Attorney General Suella Braverman was to sign it off on the utterly specious grounds that, as parliament is sovereign, it can do what it likes. This entirely ignores the government's separate obligations under international law to uphold a treaty it has signed. This was the reason for the resignation of then Treasury Solicitor and Advocate General for Scotland over the issue. It is noteworthy that Rishi Sunak, as a Prime Minister who states his commitment to upholding the rule of law, was criticised for his approach to resolving the issues around the Northern Ireland Protocol by those advocating the same flawed arguments that were used to justify the Internal Market Bill.

This also, I suggest, has corrosive effects elsewhere. Laxity in observing basic principles of the rule of law has a carry over into standards of behaviour in government. The Johnson administration quickly developed a reputation for sleaze, cronyism and dishonesty, which ultimately destroyed his premiership, and has left a damaging legacy of erosion of public trust in politicians. In 2020 Johnson decided to disregard the findings of his Ethics Adviser Sir Alex Allan and kept Priti Patel in office, despite Sir Alex's findings that she had bullied staff. This led to Sir Alex's resignation. In late 2021 Johnson then sought to overturn in the House of Commons a finding by the Parliamentary Commissioner for Standards, that Owen Paterson had engaged in paid advocacy in breach of the rules of the House. That advocacy was linked to events around the Covid pandemic, which have since produced wider allegations that the placing of multi-million-pound contracts for medical equipment during this period did not observe proper procurement procedures and favoured persons with links to ministers, as donors to the Conservative Party. Meanwhile, Johnson was allowing the draconian rules restricting social contact, which his own government had introduced to fight Covid, to be ignored by himself and his staff in his own office in Downing Street. A more recent expression of this corrosion of standards is that Nadhim Zahawi serving as Chancellor of the Exchequer did not seem to understand or appreciate that there might be an incompatibility and conflict of interest between his serving this role at the same time as being under investigation for, and found to have been involved in, tax avoidance, for which he had to pay a substantial penalty.

Reasserting the rule of law

For those of us on the liberal centre right, this erosion in Conservative principles and behaviour by governments that call themselves Conservative is a serious challenge that requires a response.

We need first to acknowledge that this erosion has not happened overnight. As public anxieties have grown in recent decades over issues such as our country's economic performance, national security, identity politics and immigration, so the temptation has grown to embrace populist policies in response. These deliberately encourage disregard for accepted standards of government behaviour and claim or at least imply that the end justifies the means. Short cuts disregarding rules and 'cakeism' have become acceptable remedies to problems. It was David Cameron who, as a prime minister, identified with the liberal centre right, started undermining the ministerial code by removing the explicit obligation of ministers to comply with international law, while admitting that it made no difference to the obligation. This was encouraged by an aggressive and demanding print media in increasing competition with the echo chamber of social media. For sections of the press an important driver has been a dislike of regulation, such as the growth in privacy law through the application of Article 8 of the ECHR by our courts, which has led to them attacking the principles of human rights law more generally. There has also been the arrival of right-wing 'think tanks' providing academic support for views on the rule of law that are well outside the mainstream and designed to justify ignoring its principles when it suits government to do so.

In the face of this, there has been a tendency for the liberal centre right to stay silent and hope the issues were just the product of irritation and could be ignored and would go away. But we are now living with the consequences. The one thing in our favour is that those consequences are proving at present, predictably, to be so entirely negative to our national well-being that sections of the electorate who had been attracted to them are appreciating that they don't work. The risk, however, is that if a better alternative from the centre right cannot be offered, those voters will either abandon the Conservative Party and turn to Labour or, much more seriously, move to the far right to seek ever more extreme change; this ignores every principle of fairness, good governance and the rule of law and is a threat to our parliamentary democracy.

We do, however, have an opportunity to reassert the centrality of the rule of law. We need to explain and be willing to debate why the observance of international obligations is so greatly in our interest and the benefits it has brought us. It lies at the heart, for example of rebuilding a credible relationship with the EU post Brexit, just as it does for any other trade agreement we might aspire to negotiate. We will need that credible relationship if the UK is to be seen once again as a good place to invest and locate businesses and as a partner that can be relied on to observe the terms of trade deals. It is also central to the lead we have taken in resisting Russian aggression and human rights violations in the Ukraine. Promoting human rights and observing them ourselves is in our self-interest. Our willingness, for example, to follow the ECtHR judgments scrupulously in the case of Abu Qatada to Jordan, despite the fury of the tabloid press and the understandable frustration of the then Home Secretary, ensured permanent statutory reforms to the Jordanian criminal justice system, which were both needed and welcomed, as well as a success in having him deported to stand a fair trial in that country.

We also need to look at why there has developed a growing gulf of understanding between politicians and those who practise law and see it as a force for good. This problem is not confined to the right, as past Labour governments have had marked problems of a similar kind, leading to confrontations between the Labour government and the courts over anti-terrorism legislation post 9/11.

Sixty years ago, the House of Commons had many practising lawyers who were familiar both with the role of judges and the operation of the law. The Lord Chancellor, who was not only a lawyer, but the most senior member of the judiciary was accorded a high status at the heart of government. The office, which was then confined to the operation of the legal system including the courts and the appointment of judges, was key to ensuring respect for the law and the maintenance of an informal dialogue between government and judiciary that served the rule of law well. Central to his standing as a judge at the heart of government was that the office was not a route for the furtherance of career ambition or judicial advancement. Today, despite the exceptional oath of office, the Lord Chancellor is absorbed in the running of the penal system as Justice Secretary, and some holders have shown scant regard for their rule of law responsibilities. The office has been diminished by the disappearance of the role of being in and Speaker of the Lords. While the role cannot be restored to what it was before 2005 and no judicial functions would now be considered proper, we should be arguing that prime ministers would benefit from ensuring that Lord Chancellors are seen as having the independence to be the key. It might be worth considering whether the functions taken over from the Home Office help or hinder the Lord Chancellor in performing his role.

Similar issues arise with the Law Officers. Their role as legal advisers should be underpinned by observance of their professional standards as lawyers. They should not, as has occurred under Johnson, have politically appointed special advisers. They and the government they serve and the government legal service should be acting and be seen to be acting with propriety, even when faced with complex challenges.

We also need to put the delivery of justice back at the centre of government priorities as a key social service of the state.

More than any other department, the Ministry of Justice has been progressively starved over 25 years – by all governments – of the funds needed to discharge its functions. The gulf between the Lord Chancellor's oath to ensure adequate resources for the courts and the actual state of court buildings and facilities, including staffing and the amounts paid to practitioners by way of Legal Aid, is now startling, despite some limited recent improvements, forced by the near total collapse of the system. Simply ensuring that the quality of justice in our highest courts is outstanding is not enough. For the public and politicians, as the system becomes slower and more dysfunctional, the sense grows of a whited sepulchre, and this too contributes to a reduction in respect for the rule of law.

The irony of the present undermining of the rule of law, is that while it has been driven by successive governments' perceived frustrations with being impeded by the law in their executive decisions, there is no evidence whatever that it has facilitated their actions at all. On the contrary it has created a conflict and an uncertainty that is inimical to governments' achieving legitimate aims within the law. A proper and constant adherence to rule of law principles would see many of the government's frustrations disappear. Those occasional frictions that would remain would be seen for what they are – a healthy manifestation of the interplay between the law, the courts and the executive. Governments would find themselves the beneficiaries of a calmer environment for making decisions and a great deal of the time currently being spent on pointless, costly and counterproductive policy projects to circumvent the rule of law would be saved. We would all be much better off. It is a deeply Conservative message that our political forebears understood very well. We need to restore it to the heart of centre right politics.

4

Fixing a Bad Brexit Deal
Gavin Barwell

No book looking at the future of the centre right would be complete without a chapter on the UK's relationship with the European Union, the issue which has so disrupted British politics over the last ten years.

Opinions on this issue, on both sides of the argument, are strongly held. It has become increasingly hard to have a rational debate about it – some blame all the ills of the country on Brexit, despite the fact that many of the UK's problems pre-date it; others regard any suggestion that Brexit has been anything other than an unalloyed success as heresy.

If we are going to try to look at this issue with an open mind, then we need to consider two things: how is the current policy working; and what do the public, particularly those voters who might support a centre right party, think? I know some readers will bridle at the second question. Why, they will ask, can't you just think about what's best for the country for once? But political parties aren't think tanks or pressure groups. They exist to win elections: if they don't do that, they can't put any of their ideas into practice. Of course, the starting point should always be what's right for the country, but that has to be tempered by an assessment of what is politically possible. The best politicians have always known when to lead public opinion and when to follow it.

So, this chapter will start with an assessment of what impact the particular form of Brexit that Boris Johnson chose has had on our economy, our own Union, our standing in the world and our relations with our nearest neighbours. It will then look at what the public thinks and how that is likely to evolve, before ending with some suggestions about what those two things suggest the centre right should do now. But it may be helpful to begin with a brief look at how we got here.

How we got here

As Tim Marshall argues in his book *Prisoners of Geography*, the UK's relationship with Europe has been shaped by its geography – 'close enough to the European continent to trade and yet protected by dint of being an island'. As a result, we learned a different lesson from the Second World War than continental Europeans. For them, the lesson was that nationalism had to be suppressed to avoid another European war; for us, it was that our national spirit had allowed us to fight on alone. And so, when they formed the European Coal and Steel Community after the war, which then morphed into the European Economic Community, we sat on the sidelines.

But we found that didn't work for us economically, so the Conservative Party, first under Macmillan and then successfully under Heath, supported the UK joining. From the outset, there were some Eurosceptics who took a different view but, in a free vote in April 1975, 249 out of 275 Conservative MPs voted in favour of membership. In 1983, the Conservative manifesto, in what would be branded as Project Fear today, said that Labour's policy of withdrawal would be:

... a catastrophe for this country. As many as two million jobs would be at risk. We would lose the great export advantages and the attraction to overseas investors which membership now gives us. It would be a fateful step towards isolation, at which only the Soviet Union and her allies would rejoice.

And, in a speech at Mansion House in 1988, Margaret Thatcher lauded the single market that she played a pivotal role in creating:

A single market without barriers – visible or invisible – giving direct and unhindered access to the purchasing power of over 300 million of the world's wealthiest and most prosperous people. Bigger than Japan. Bigger than the United States. On your doorstep. Europe wasn't open for business. Underneath the rhetoric, the old barriers remained. Not just against the outside world, but between European countries. Not the classic barriers of tariffs, but the insidious ones of differing national standards, various restrictions on the provision of services, exclusion of foreign firms from public contracts. Now that's going to change.

Note her focus on the economic harm of non-tariff barriers to trade: these are precisely the barriers that Johnson's Brexit deal has introduced and from which our economy is now suffering.

So, what happened? Why did the Conservative Party switch from strongly supporting membership, albeit with various rebates and opt-outs along the way, to supporting Brexit? You could write a whole book just on that question but, I think, there were four key moments. First, Europe changed (or perhaps more accurately developed in a way that had always been intended, but which caught the UK – which hadn't been paying attention – by surprise). The Delors Commission pushed for greater political union and, in particular, for the adoption of a single currency. The UK chose to stay out but now it had a problem: the danger that the EU would be dominated by those countries in the eurozone in a way that would work contrary to British interests. And more and more Conservatives felt uncomfortable with the sheer volume of law that was being made at a European level. Second, the accession of a number of eastern European countries and the failure of the Blair government to impose accession controls on free movement led to very high levels of immigration. This was the issue that allowed those who had always been opposed to our membership to mobilise mass support. Third, the emergence of UKIP under Nigel Farage was a serious electoral threat; that led Conservative MPs (yours truly included) to pressure David Cameron into promising a referendum on our membership. Our electoral system played a key role here. In a proportional system, UKIP polling ten per cent would not have posed a serious threat to the Conservative Party, but in a first-past-the-post system it would have made it impossible to win marginal seats like mine. And fourth, was the referendum result itself. In 2016, just over half the Conservative Party campaigned for Remain but, having chosen to pass the decision to the British people, the vast majority (rightly in my opinion) felt honour bound to respect their choice.

That leaves one final thing to explain: why did we end up with this particular form of Brexit? This is a key question because, contrary to what some people would have you believe, all Brexits are not the same: there is a world of difference, both in terms of barriers to trade and the freedoms the UK would have, between at one extreme staying in the single market and customs union and, at the other extreme, leaving with no deal. You could write another whole book on this question (in fact, I have) but, in brief, the 2017 election left Theresa May without a majority. There were only two ways for her to get Brexit done: either via a cross-party deal (difficult in our adversarial system at the best of times and even more so with Labour led by Jeremy Corbyn), or with the near unanimous support of Conservative and DUP MPs. Whether you blame Theresa May, Jeremy Corbyn, Keir Starmer and those pushing for a second referendum, or all of the above, those MPs who were opposed to a 'hard' Brexit were unable to unite around any single alternative, killing off any prospect of a cross-party deal. The right of the Conservative Party refused to back the compromise deal Theresa negotiated, which they saw as Brexit in name only, and replaced her with Boris Johnson (who in three years had been transformed from a pro-European to the hardest of Brexiteers). He promptly sold out Northern Ireland, agreeing to the version of the Northern Ireland Protocol that the EU had wanted all along which introduced a partial border between Great Britain and Northern Ireland, and was able to achieve the majority at the 2019 election that Theresa should have achieved in 2017.

What does 'here' look like?

Before discussing its impact, it's probably also helpful to include a very brief description of Boris Johnson's Brexit deal. Economically, the best thing that can be said about that is that it ensures there are no tariffs or quotas on the import and export of any goods (provided they meet what are known as rules of origin requirements). However, it introduces significant non-tariff barriers to trade of the kind Margaret Thatcher warned about, in the form of customs declarations and regulatory and customs checks when goods move between Great Britain and the EU, and reduces the ability of our services sector to access the EU market. As mentioned above, it also introduces a partial border when goods move within the United Kingdom from Great Britain to Northern Ireland, breaking up the UK's single market.

When it comes to foreign and defence policy, there is no formal relationship between the UK and the EU, although we still work together on an *ad hoc* basis on issues like Ukraine. The Political Declaration that formed part of Johnson's oven-ready deal said that there should be 'appropriate dialogue, consultation, coordination, exchange of information and cooperation mechanisms' on these issues but, when the deal emerged from the oven, these mechanisms had disappeared.

Has Brexit been a success?

The answer to this question is inevitably contested, in part because people on both sides believe so strongly that we made the right or the wrong decision that they tune out evidence that doesn't support their view and in part because people don't agree on what success would look like.

For some people, Brexit was about getting back control of our laws. On this basis, with the partial exception of Northern Ireland, it has been a success; indeed, it couldn't fail to be a success. But most people take a more practical view: their tests of success are whether Brexit has made us more or less prosperous, strengthened or weakened our Union and increased or diminished our influence in the world. Against these tests, the assessment is less positive. Let's start with the economy because Liz Truss was right (there are four words you don't hear very often): the biggest challenge facing our politicians is the low underlying growth rate of our economy ever since the Global Financial Crisis. The fact that this problem stretches back to 2008 tells you that Brexit is not the sole source of our woes, but has it made things better, worse or made no difference?

Before trying to answer that question we need to start with an acknowledgement: it is impossible to quantify the impact precisely. By definition, we are trying to compare what has happened since we left with what we think would have happened had we stayed in the EU. The latter can only ever be an estimate, and that estimate will only be as good as the assumptions on which it is based. And the impact is harder to see because a global pandemic with huge economic impacts took place in the middle of the process.

Nevertheless, with those caveats in mind, the Centre for European Reform has produced such an estimate based on a 'doppelganger' in which an algorithm models how the UK's economy would have performed if it remained within the EU using data from economies that closely matched the UK's prior to Brexit. Their central prediction is that UK GDP was 5.5 per cent smaller in June 2022 than it would have been if we had stayed in the EU (to be clear, they are not saying that the economy has shrunk by 5.5 per cent; they are saying it has grown by less than it would have done). Because this is only an estimate, not a statement of fact, they actually published a range – the 5th centile showed the economy three per cent smaller than it would have been; the 95th centile showed it 6.7 per cent smaller. In other words, we can say with a high degree of confidence that we are poorer than we would have been, but with some debate about the exact scale of the impact.

Figure 4.1 suggests that some of the economic damage happened pretty quickly – after we had voted to leave, but before we had actually left – suggesting it would have happened whatever version of Brexit we had ultimately chosen; the rest happened after the end of the transition period, suggesting it was the result of the particular model of Brexit Boris Johnson opted for.

The report has predictably been dismissed as the work of the Remain establishment but, rather than do that, Conservative MPs should take a closer look because it explains a paradox that they are currently very concerned about: tax rates are not that high by historical standards, but the tax burden – tax raised as a percentage of our GDP – is close to a post-war high. How can both these things be true? Because our economy hasn't grown by as much as it should have done; the 'cake' is smaller than it should be, so a bigger slice of that cake is

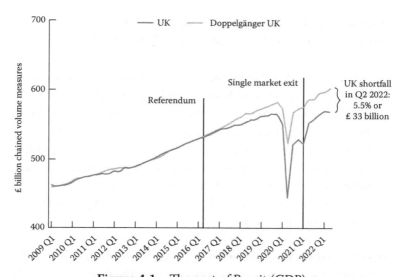

Figure 4.1   The cost of Brexit (GDP)
Source: John Springford, 'The cost of Brexit to June 2022', The Centre for
European Reform, 21 December 2022.

needed to fund a given level of public services. If our economy
were 5.5 per cent bigger, tax revenues would be about £40 billion higher. If Conservatives want a lower tax burden, there are
only three ways of getting it: borrow more (tried that, didn't
work out too well), spend less (but public services like the
NHS arguably need more money right now, not less) or grow
more. And if grow more is the only answer then, painful as it
will be for many of them, Conservative MPs have to look at
the economic harm that Brexit has done. As I will explore at
the end of this chapter that doesn't have to mean abandoning
Brexit, but it does mean rethinking the current deal.

That economic harm has at least three components. First,
and hopefully least controversially, the impact on trade. If
Conservative MPs believe that lowering barriers to trade with
countries like Australia has economic benefits, they cannot
credibly argue that raising them with our nearest neighbours,
with whom we have much larger volumes of trade, doesn't

have a cost. The Bank of England certainly thinks so, here is what it said in its *February Monetary Policy Report*:

> Barriers to trade between the UK and EU have increased, and that is likely to result in lower trade between the UK and EU than there would have otherwise been. Around the time that the UK left the EU, these effects were expected to leave the level of productivity 3.25 per cent lower in the long run, given productivity's well-established relationship with openness. In the current forecast more of the previously estimated effect on productivity takes effect by the end of the forecast period than was the case previously.

In other words, the Bank is seeing what it expected to see, but it is happening a bit quicker. Figure 4.2 tells the story very clearly (the dotted line is the correct comparison – the official data have been adjusted to take account of a change in the source of the UK's goods trade data, which has moved from a survey of companies to customs declarations, and an adjustment for an inflation of goods imports from the EU in the first half of 2022, caused by delayed customs declarations from the second

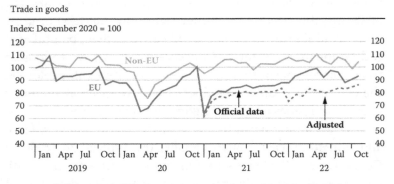

Figure 4.2   The impact on goods trade with the EU

Source: Bank of England, *Monetary Policy Report – February 2023*, Chart 3.6. Data and calculations from the Bank of England and ONS.

half of 2021). It shows very clearly that, whereas both EU and non-EU trade were impacted by the onset of the pandemic, only EU trade fell at the end of the transition period, when the barriers to trade were introduced, and shows no signs of fully recovering.

The second harm is to investment. Here is the Bank of England from its *February Monetary Policy Report* again:

> It is likely that Brexit has been affecting investment for some time. Business investment has been very subdued. This reflects a variety of factors, but some of the stalling after 2016 probably reflects the effects of Brexit as resources were diverted to Brexit preparations and uncertainty around future trading relationships reduced capital spending.

As you can see from Figure 4.3, the impact here is felt as soon as we voted to leave, rather than after the end of the transition period.

And the final impact is on the labour market. Research by Professor Jonathan Portes of King's College London and John Springford, the deputy director of the Centre for European

Business investment

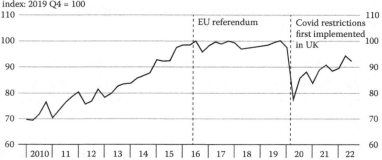

Figure 4.3 The impact on business investment

Source: Bank of England, *Monetary Policy Report – February 2023*, Chart 3.7. Data and calculations from the Bank of England and ONS.

Reform, suggests that the end of free movement has led to a shortfall of around 330,000 workers in Britain, about one per cent of the labour force. They arrived at this figure by estimating how many EU and non-EU workers would have been in employment if free movement had not ended and Britain's immigration laws had remained as they were before the new system started in January 2021, and then comparing that counterfactual to what has actually happened, as measured by the Annual Population Survey. This showed that by June 2022 there was a significant shortfall of around 460,000 EU-origin workers, partly but not wholly compensated for by an increase of about 130,000 non-EU workers. There is a very varied impact by sector – there are big net shortfalls in less-skilled sectors of the economy, whereas in more skilled sectors such as healthcare, education and ICT an increase in non-EU workers has more than compensated for losses of those from the EU. The researchers make the point that it will take time for employers to respond to these shortages, and predict some combination of higher wages (good) and prices (bad) and less output (bad), especially in work that is hard to automate.

It is then pretty clear that thus far Brexit has made us poorer as a country than we would otherwise have been. Even some Brexit supporters, like Julian Jessop, a fellow at the Institute for Economic Affairs, acknowledge this, although they argue that things might improve in time:

> We're still in a sort of transition phase, where the negatives are dominating [but those negatives are] more likely to be temporary, because a lot of them have to do with uncertainty and the process of adjustment.

But if the impact on our economy is contested even though clear, the impact on our Union is undeniable. The partial border down the Irish Sea that Boris Johnson signed up to is bitterly resented by Unionists. It has led to the DUP pulling out of various strands of the Good Friday Agreement, including the collapse of devolved government. At the time of writing, it is still not clear if the improvements Rishi Sunak secured in the Windsor Framework will be enough to get the institutions back up and running. Conservative MPs complain that the EU has been unreasonable, but all it has asked is for the UK to implement the deal they all voted for and told their constituents was a great deal back in 2019! And, in Scotland, Brexit has allowed the SNP to push for a second referendum, arguing – with some legitimacy – that something fundamental has changed since 2014. Many Unionists celebrated Nicola Sturgeon's resignation in February 2023 and the subsequent difficulties faced by the SNP, believing that the independence genie is now back in its lamp. Although the imminent threat has certainly receded, given the very strong age skew when it comes to support for independence believing the argument is now settled feels like a very optimistic take.

The impact on our standing in the world is harder to quantify. Most of the foreign politicians and diplomats to whom I have spoken are baffled by the decision we have taken, although some saw opportunities for their own countries – our government is, or at least was, clearly in a hurry to do trade deals with others to demonstrate the benefits of Brexit – and they sensed an opportunity to extract concessions (I was interested to hear the former DEFRA Secretary George Eustice admit that the Australia deal 'is not actually a very good deal for the UK'). The spectacle of the UK government threatening to breach its international commitments was hugely damaging to our international reputation, and will be quoted back to us by those we seek to hold to account for years to come. But it is important not to overstate things: on Ukraine, for example, we have played a leadership role that is widely respected (there is an irony – but also something admirable – about Boris Johnson's passion to secure Ukraine's freedom to join an institution he fought so hard to take the UK out of).

Our relationship with our immediate neighbours has almost inevitably been damaged. Partly this stems from the amount of time they have had to devote to negotiations with the UK due to the turbulence in our politics since the referendum. But far worse has been the loss of trust in the UK after the Johnson government negotiated a deal in bad faith, then refused to implement it, and then brought forward domestic legislation to unilaterally overturn some of it. It is going to take time to rebuild that faith, and that has consequences for what the centre right should do next, which I shall discuss at the end of this chapter; but Rishi Sunak has made a good start.

What do the public and business think?

Most economists, constitutional experts and foreign-policy analysts may think that Brexit has damaged our economy, our Union, our standing in the world and our relationship with our nearest neighbours, but what do the British people think? After all, if it had been left to the experts, we would never have left the EU in the first place.

YouGov have run a tracker poll ever since the referendum, asking people whether in hindsight they think Britain was right or wrong to leave. As Figure 4.4 shows, for about five years there was very little fluctuation – most of the time, slightly more people said we were wrong to leave than right but the gap was within the margin of error. And then, just under two years ago, the gap started to open up and bit by bit it has widened. The last time YouGov asked the question, only 32 per cent thought we made the right decision; 56 per cent – nearly twice as many – thought we had made a mistake.

That is a big gap – big enough, it turns out, to overcome the geographic variation in support for Brexit. Another pollster – *Focaldata* – recently conducted a poll with a much larger

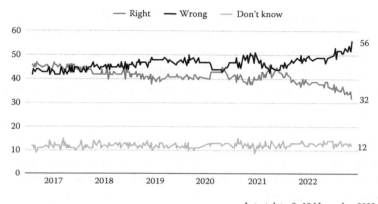

Latest date: 9–10 November 2022

Figure 4.4   Public opinion: In hindsight, do you think Britain was right or wrong to vote to leave the European Union? (%)
Source: YouGov Plc 2022 © All rights reserved.

sample for *UnHerd*. The larger sample size allowed them to model the result in every constituency in the country, and what they found is that there is only one constituency in England, Scotland or Wales (Boston and Skegness in Lincolnshire) where more people disagree with the statement 'Britain was wrong to leave the EU' than agree with it (there are two others, also in Lincolnshire, where it's neck and neck).[1]

And what's more pollsters expect the gap to continue to widen. There are two things driving the divergence:

- First, demographic change: elderly people die off and are replaced by new young voters and, given the very significant age skew when it comes to attitudes to Brexit, that means the balance of opinion changes even if no one changes their minds. Demographic change is obviously going to continue. It is of course possible that people will become more Eurosceptic as they get older in the same way as they tend to become a bit more Conservative as they get older, but there is no sign of that at present; and

- second, people changing their minds: to date, many more Leave voters have decided we made a mistake than Remain voters who now think Brexit was a good idea. And pollsters think that trend too might continue – at the moment at least, there are more soft 'Right decision' voters than 'Wrong decision' ones.

This poses a profound electoral risk to the Conservative Party. It is heavily associated with a policy which is making it harder for it to deliver the low tax economy it believes in and which a growing majority of voters think was a mistake. Brexit is in danger of becoming the Conservative Party's version of unilateral nuclear disarmament – a policy that a minority of the electorate passionately support, but which most voters think is not in the national interest. As time goes by the percentage of the electorate who won't vote Conservative if the party sticks to its current policy is going to grow and grow.

But there are two important caveats.

First, regret does not, as yet at any rate, equal rejoin. Given the high levels of regret, another pollster, *JL Partners*, conducted a poll to try to find out what people think we should do now. It found that only seven per cent of voters – and just ten per cent of Leavers – want to stick with the current deal. 51 per cent – including 43 per cent of Leavers – want a closer relationship than we have now. But only 23 per cent want to rejoin the EU; eleven per cent want to rejoin the single market but not the EU; and seventeen per cent want a closer trade partnership than today but outside the single market (in the interests of balance, seven per cent of voters and thirteen per cent of Leavers want no or minimal economic ties with the EU).[2] So, we can say with confidence that the deal that Johnson and Frost negotiated is not going to stick, that the public have made up their minds that they want a closer relationship, but they are divided about how close exactly.

The second caveat is that centre right voters are more likely still to think Brexit was a good idea – the *Focaldata/ UnHerd* poll found that enthusiasm for Brexit has faded more in left-leaning areas than in Tory heartlands. If those of us who think that the Conservative Party's current policy is not in the national or its own interest are to have a chance of persuading our colleagues, we need to acknowledge that so far it has worked in the party's favour; both in 2017 (when, despite running a very bad campaign and losing some seats, the party secured an additional 2.3 million votes, mainly in Leave voting areas) and 2019 (when it secured a further 300,000 votes and, due to the collapse in the Labour vote, gained nearly 50 seats); and that the party is now caught in a trap of its own making: if it abandoned Brexit altogether, it would probably lose more votes to Reform than it gains, but if it continues to support the current deal that is going to become an increasing electoral millstone round its neck. I will discuss how to get out of this trap in the last section of this chapter.

But, before doing that, it is important to note that Brexit isn't just increasingly unpopular with the general public, but also with the party's natural supporters in the business community. Research for the British Chambers of Commerce found more than three-quarters of the firms trading with the EU find the existing Brexit deal no help at all when it comes to increasing sales or growing their businesses. More than half are still struggling to get their heads around new goods rules, and almost half are struggling to work out new services rules.

Boris Johnson famously declared 'F**k business' when someone raised business concerns about Brexit with him, but no centre right politician should take that attitude. People who build and grow businesses create the wealth on which the country depends, and their views on what makes it easier or harder to grow their businesses should be listened to. And, at the next election, the party will need to convince the electorate that it, not Labour, will do a better job of managing the economy. It will be much harder to do that if business leaders are increasingly hostile to the party because it is openly contemptuous of their views on trade with the EU. I was struck by a quote from a department head at a major investment bank that I read in *Politico* the other day:

> The biggest danger in British politics right now is the right of the Tory Party, not the left of the Labour Party. I like Rishi, but he is leading a party that is dysfunctional and ideological.

It is very hard to argue with that assessment.

So what to do?

As discussed, Boris Johnson's Brexit deal has introduced significant barriers to trade, harming our economy, and straining our Union. His willingness to break the commitments we had freely entered into damaged our standing in the world and compounded the damage to our relationship with our nearest neighbours. Rishi Sunak has begun the process of rebuilding trust, and the Windsor Framework reduces the damage to the UK single market, but it doesn't change the overall trading and security relationship with the EU at all.

And the exceptionalism of our position is only going to increase over time. One of the geopolitical consequences of the war in Ukraine is that the enlargement of the EU, which had been very much in the long grass, is now back on. If Ukraine can secure its independence then, a decade from now it, Moldova and the countries of the western Balkans and possibly Georgia are likely to be members of the EU. At that point, the UK will be the only major European country that is not in the EU or its single market (Switzerland isn't technically in the single market, but it effectively has access thanks to a series of bilateral agreements).

In terms of public opinion, less than ten per cent of the electorate want to stick with the current deal but, although an increasing majority of the electorate regret Brexit, those who do still support it are disproportionately Conservative supporters. And there is not yet, and there may never be, a majority in favour of rejoining. Nor should we assume that the EU would necessarily have us back – certainly not on the old terms and certainly not if there was a risk that we might change our minds again. This argues for a gradualist approach, recognising that the current relationship is not in the national interest, identifying how to improve it without rejoining and seeing how public opinion evolves over time.

The starting point is to rebuild trust. As previously noted, Rishi Sunak has made a start on this. The EU will now be watching very closely to see if this time the UK implements the things it has committed to. But, even now, after all the damage that has been done to our economy, our Union, our standing in the world and our relationships with our neighbours, there were some who were urging Sunak to proceed with the Northern Ireland Protocol Bill that breaks this country's word, overriding a treaty into which we freely entered. Such a strategy would not have extracted further concessions from the EU; why would they do another deal with a country that has proved itself untrustworthy? It would only have further damaged the relationship and further harmed our economy. It would also have further undermined electoral support for Brexit because it would have shown very clearly that, contrary to Boris Johnson's promises back in 2019, there was no oven-ready deal and Brexit would have remained not completely done.

There is one further point on restoring trust that those on the centre right need to face up to: it is harder for the Conservative Party to do so than Labour or a new centre right party. European leaders certainly see Rishi Sunak as an improvement on Boris Johnson or Liz Truss, but they know that he is constrained by the need to keep his parliamentary party united. For, so long as the Conservative Party contains people who are not just Brexiteers but hostile to the continued existence of the EU, then trust is going to be in relatively low supply.

Beyond resolving the long-running sore of the Northern Ireland Protocol, what else could be done to rebuild trust? A good starting point would be to implement what Boris Johnson agreed on cooperation mechanisms on foreign and security policy. Ukraine has shown that we can find ways to cooperate on an *ad hoc* basis in an emergency, but it has also underlined the ongoing need for that co-operation. There are some fundamental truths that we need to recognise:

- you can take the UK out of the EU, but you can't take it out of Europe, and the UK and EU's shared geography and values mean they face the same threats – when it comes to Russia, China, migration or climate change, their interests are very much aligned; and
- the scale of those threats is such that the UK and EU can only overcome them by working together.

In April 2023, President Macron gave an ill-judged interview on his way back from a visit to China in which he essentially implied that Europe should not align with the US over Taiwan ('The worst thing would be to think that we Europeans need to be followers about this and adapt ourselves to the American rhythm and a Chinese overreaction'). We failed to deter Russia over Ukraine and both the Ukrainians and the global economy are paying the price for that; his remarks risk repeating the mistake with China over Taiwan. But, as ever with Macron, he has an underlying point about the risks of Europeans depending on the US for our defence. The question we and the EU need to ask ourselves is how would we have responded to the Russian invasion of Ukraine if, instead of Joe Biden, we'd had a President who took the view that the territorial integrity of Ukraine was not a strategic interest of the United States? Currently, that seems to be the position of Donald Trump and Ron DeSantis, the two leading contenders for the Republican nomination for the next presidential election. And, even if Biden wins again next time, over time the US focus is inevitably going to shift increasingly to the Pacific. Europeans are going to have to take a greater responsibility for their collective defence from Putin and his successors.

However, it is not just the threat from Russia. The pandemic and the economic consequences of the war in Ukraine have pushed a number of countries into financial distress. Over time, climate change will act as a crisis multiplier. One consequence is likely to be increased migration. We can try to stop small boats crossing the Channel, and the EU can try to stop them crossing the Mediterranean, but desperate people will seek a better life somewhere else. If we want to prevent large movements of people then we need to work together to stabilise and support economic growth in the countries in our near abroad from which people are emigrating. And if we want to stop the worst impacts of climate change then, as countries that are at the forefront of the move to a net zero economy, we need to collaborate closely in the COP process.

Nor is the need for collaboration limited to geopolitics. If we want to keep people safe from both ordinary criminals and terrorists, we need to rebuild to the maximum extent possible the collaboration between our law enforcement agencies and judicial authorities, which was lost when we left the EU.

In other words, given the extent of the shared threats we need more than *ad hoc* co-operation. An annual UK/EU summit would be a good starting point. With the exception of those they meet in E3, G7 or G20 formats, UK ministers and officials don't spend much time with their opposite numbers from the 27 anymore. An annual summit would build those personal relationships; but it would need to be a separate event, not tagged on as an afterthought to a European Council, with the terrible optics of the Brits leaving as the others get on with the main business. We should also explore what role the new European Political Community could play in a closer relationship; Liz Truss deserves credit for agreeing to take part in this format. But ultimately, we need the kind of specific mechanisms that were envisaged in both the May and Johnson Brexit deals, but which the Johnson government chose not to take forward.

Turning to the crucial economic relationship, we need to face up to a hard truth: there is a limit to how much of the economic harm done by the Johnson deal you can undo unless you are willing to enter into a customs union and/or rejoin the single market. Back in November, Jeremy Hunt said:

> I think having unfettered trade with our neighbours – and countries all over the world – is very beneficial to growth. I have great confidence that over the years ahead we will find, outside the single market, we are able to remove the vast majority of the trade barriers that exist between us and the EU.

It was great to hear a Conservative minister be clear that barriers to trade with the EU are a bad thing, but I don't share his confidence (apart from perhaps in the long term when, at some point, AI may significantly reduce the volume of friction at borders between all friendly states). If you are not in a customs union with the EU, then UK exports and EU imports are going to require customs declarations and face customs checks. And the EU is not going to waive regulatory checks on a country outside its single market – why would it allow anyone to enjoy the benefits of single market membership without the obligations?

There is not yet public support for rejoining the single market, but we should consider the case for a customs union. That decision should be driven not by an absolutist view of sovereignty, but a pragmatic assessment of the national interest. Being in a customs union with the EU would place constraints on the type of trade deals we can do with third countries, but it is absurd to suggest that it would represent Brexit In Name Only. Turkey is in a customs union in the EU – no one would suggest that it is therefore effectively a member of the EU. The question we need to ask is whether the constraints membership of a customs union would place on the trade deals we have done or might realistically do outweigh the combination of the benefits of the equivalent deals the EU is doing or might do, plus the savings to the British economy from the removal of customs declarations and checks on trade with the EU.

If we are not prepared to rejoin the single market or the customs union, what low-hanging fruit is there? There are some immediate benefits that should flow now that we have resolved the long-running dispute over the Northern Ireland Protocol: a Memorandum of Understanding on financial services regulation, a deal on electricity trading, UK participation in the Horizon research and innovation programme. Beyond that, we need to look at some of the things the EU offered in the negotiations leading to the Johnson deal that David Frost rejected (greater access to each other's audiovisual markets, a deal on youth mobility, UK participation in the Erasmus+ education programme) and some of the arrangements the EU has with other third countries (something similar to the EU/New Zealand veterinary agreement, a similar level of co-ordination on financial services to that which the EU has with the US, UK participation in the EU/US Trade and Technology Council).

Nevertheless, the key is we need to have an overall vision for the relationship we want, rather than addressing these issues one by one. There are some that the EU will be very keen on, and others that will be harder to negotiate. The Johnson deal contains numerous review clauses, both of specific elements of the deal and of the overall relationship. Right now, the EU regards the latter as a formality, but it will be preparing for the former, thinking about what it wants to get out of each of them. Given that as the larger partner it has the stronger hand in these negotiations – another hard truth we need to recognise now that we are outside: we do not hold all the cards – if we don't have an attractive and credible vision for how the economic and security relationship could be improved to the benefit of both parties, the current deal could actually get a bit worse (think, for example, of the forthcoming end of the temporary exemption of rules of origin requirements on electric vehicles).

Conclusion

An objective analysis shows that Boris Johnson's Brexit deal, and his subsequent attempts to wriggle out of parts of it, has harmed our economy, our Union, our standing in the world and our relationships with our closest neighbours. Conservatives and Unionists should care about all of these things. The exceptionalism of our current position is only likely to increase over time as Ukraine, Moldova and countries in the western Balkans join. Recent events in Ukraine have demonstrated that the UK and EU's shared geography and values mean their interests are strongly aligned. And polling shows only a very small minority of the electorate want to stick with the current deal. In both the national and its own interest, the Conservative Party needs to wake up and smell the coffee.

But that same polling also shows there is not a majority for rejoining. The right response is therefore not to re-open the whole Brexit debate, but to think about how the deal could be improved. We should do that thinking free from ideology, whether of the europhile or europhobe variety, driven by the pragmatic focus on what is in the national interest that used to characterize the centre right in the UK, and was its secret weapon.

5

A Renewed Agenda for Conservative Economics

Tim Pitt

For the best part of half a century, Conservative economic thinking dominated the UK political and policy agenda. Putting financial discipline and free markets at the centre of its approach, Margaret Thatcher's government delivered a raft of reforms designed to unpick what it saw as the ever-increasing state intervention and financial indiscipline that had characterised the Butskellite post-war consensus.

In doing so, Thatcher not only changed the course of the UK economy but also heavily influenced thinking across the political spectrum, domestically and internationally. While the Conservatives were swept away by the 1997 landslide, their economics were not: Thatcher famously described Tony Blair and New Labour as her 'greatest achievement'.[1]

Yet recent years have seen slower growth, sharply rising public debt, huge pressure on public services, high inequality and an historically protracted squeeze on living standards. This has brought the Thatcherite consensus firmly into the firing line, with its perceived failures coming under attack from both the left and populist right. Both share the view that the UK's economic model is fundamentally broken.

Looking forward, the coming decades will continue to

be played out on challenging territory for Conservatives. Demographic and other pressures will put more strain on both public services and the public finances. Structural forces mean the UK will also probably see both lower growth than the decades leading up to the financial crisis and further upward pressure on economic inequality. Left unchecked, this combination will lead to continued public dissatisfaction with our economic model, leaving the door open to populists offering simple sounding solutions to complex problems. The challenge for Conservatives, therefore, is to produce a refreshed economic platform that adapts to and addresses these headwinds, while staying true to its core principles. That is what this chapter will attempt to outline.

In doing so, Conservatism must reject the argument that the UK's recent economic challenges are simply the result of the failure of centre right economics, and resist the temptation to be dragged towards radical populist solutions. Conservatives should be inherently sceptical about such solutions, believing as they do in the importance of stability and of managing change carefully, and cognisant that history tells us that radical overhaul often does more harm than good. The Conservative Party has forgotten this in recent years, notably with the type of Brexit it pursued and the fiscal policy with which it disastrously flirted under Liz Truss, in both cases grounded in a combination of mis-remembered version of Thatcherism and a complete ignorance of a much longer, richer history of Conservative thinking.

Yet there are reasons for optimism. The silver lining in the various recent attempts we have seen at simple sounding radical reform has been that they have revealed all too clearly the trade-offs inherent in economic policymaking, which their proponents on both right and left have invariably dismissed. The impacts of the Brexit path the UK chose have become increasingly clear, while the 2022 UK fiscal crisis put paid to the politically fashionable idea that concerns about the sustainability of the public finances could just be ignored. In doing so, renewed political space has been created for the type of pragmatic, solutions-focused policymaking that should be the basis of any centre right economic agenda.

This must not be confused, however, with a lack of ambition. Calling out populist proposals for what they are does not mean retreating into do-nothing managerialism. While there are structural headwinds we cannot wish away, policy can make a material difference and change is required. Conservative economics needs a refresh because, while the central tenets of the Thatcherite playbook are sound – free markets, financial discipline and scepticism of state intervention – they were designed for the challenges of half a century ago and are insufficient on their own to meet those facing the UK economy today. The focus instead must be on dealing with longstanding problems that successive governments have lacked the political will to deal with, such as the complexity of our tax and planning systems, as well as tackling newer and emerging problems, such as climate change and our ageing population.

In seeking to establish a renewed framework for Conservative economics, this chapter will start by establishing a high-level set of principles to be drawn on, grounded in Conservatism's rich economic history. It will then analyse the main challenges facing the UK economy over the coming decades, and conclude by setting out some practical policy suggestions to tackle them, grounded in those longstanding principles.

Principles for Conservative economics

Since 2016 Conservative economic policy has lurched one way then another under a series of leaders with fundamentally different views on economics, many of them bearing little resemblance to traditional Conservatism. Theresa May and Boris Johnson both distanced themselves from the orthodox

economic policy of the David Cameron era, acknowledging
that the economy was not working as it should and proposing
a range of fixes: May by adopting an explicitly more statist
approach, pledging to fix 'broken markets' and attacking
business; Johnson by saying he was never comfortable with
austerity, significantly increasing public spending and delivering the hardest of Brexits. Both of their attacks on the status
quo were relatively modest compared to the all-out assault
launched by Liz Truss during her brief time as Prime Minister,
attacking as she did the 'abacus economics that the Treasury
orthodoxy has promoted for years . . . [which] hasn't worked in
our economy because what we have ended up with is high tax,
high spending and low growth'.[2] Rishi Sunak has subsequently
brought some much-needed stability. But coming to power
twelve years after the Conservatives returned to government
and with a restless parliamentary party, it has been difficult to
embed a sense of Conservative economic renewal. The sense
that the party still lacks a clear economic agenda remains.

A central reason for this is that the Conservative Party has
become disconnected from its history. Perhaps more than any
other political philosophy, Conservatism's belief in organi-
cism, tradition and institutions means its approach should
be grounded in its past. Yet the contemporary debate on
Conservative economics focuses obsessively on a few specific
areas, notably the tax burden and the size of the state, taking
for granted what a 'Conservative' approach should be without
any historical context. To the extent the debate does engage
with Conservative history, it tends to take a highly selective
approach. The leadership campaign to replace Boris Johnson
serves as a classic example, with nearly all the candidates
pitching themselves as Thatcherites on platforms of unfunded
tax cuts that would have horrified Margaret Thatcher. At least
Thatcher continues to feature in the debate: there is virtually
no discussion of any other period of Conservative economics.

Any renewed Conservative economic framework must correct these failings, grounding itself in its much broader history.

Conservative economic thinking has evolved significantly over the last two hundred years. Its modern origins can be traced back to Robert Peel's liberalising reforms, which established the importance of free markets and free trade in Conservative thought. Yet this was never absolute: indeed, the party then went through a prolonged period of scepticism towards *laissez-faire* economics, willing to accept a greater role for the state under Benjamin Disraeli, as the party embraced social reform to deal with the fallout from the Industrial Revolution. This scepticism lasted well into the twentieth century; it was only with the replacement of the Liberals by the Labour Party as the second major force in British politics after 1918 that Conservatism began to define itself against socialism and warn more explicitly of the dangers of an over-mighty state. Nevertheless, following the Second World War Conservatism quickly made its peace with the enormous increase in the state's size that Clement Attlee's introduction of the welfare state ushered in. It was only with Thatcher's ascension to power that the reduction of the state became central.

This evolution reflects both the broad church which Conservatism has always represented, as well as the changing nature of the economic challenges it has had to confront. Yet, through this evolution, it is nevertheless possible to divine a set of four enduring principles that have consistently been part of the Conservative economic approach, principles which illustrate both how Conservative economics is distinguishable from the economics of the left, as well as how recent Tory governments have become unmoored from historic Conservative economics.

Pragmatism

The first is self-evident from the scale of the evolution described above: Conservatism has been pragmatic, willing to confront trade-offs and ground its approach in realism. In doing so, it has been deeply sceptical of ideology, instead adapting its views to meet the challenges of the day. As Arthur Balfour, Conservative Prime Minister at the beginning of the last century, put it, 'the field of economic theory . . . depends for its content on such variable elements as custom, law, knowledge, social organisation; nay on human nature itself which . . . is not necessarily the same from generation to generation . . . Every phase of civilisation requires its own political economy.'[3] Indeed, one of Conservatism's historic roles has been to act as the counter to ideology: to *laissez-faire* liberalism in the nineteenth century and to socialism in the twentieth.

Jeremy Corbyn's time as leader of the Labour Party serves as a reminder of the persistence of ideology in large sections of the British left. Yet in recent times the Conservative Party has also forgotten this pragmatic principle. The Johnson administration's refusal to confront the trade-offs inherent in Brexit and the Truss government's disastrous flirtation with libertarian ideology are both examples of the Conservative Party rejecting the pragmatism that has been a core part of its essence for over two centuries.

This does not mean that bold, significant reform is not periodically required. From Peel's dismantling of protection to Thatcher's reforms of the 1980s, Conservatism has driven economic reform when necessary. But it has done so carefully and thoughtfully, and by confronting trade-odds rather than ignoring them.

Stewardship

These reforms also serve as examples of the second principle of Conservative economics: that of stewardship, rooted in Edmund Burke's belief that 'a state without the means of some change is without the means of its own conservation'.[4] Conservatism has seen change as necessary to drive economic progress, but has also recognised that abrupt change poses a threat to the stability it holds dear. The task has therefore been to manage change carefully. In doing so, the maintenance of established customs and institutions has been central, as has been the need to move gradually: both Peel and Thatcher's reforms were implemented in stages.

But recent Conservatism has failed to abide by the stewardship principle. It has managed economic change badly, notably by failing to support those communities most affected by deindustrialisation and by its pursuit of the most disruptive of Brexits. It has also been openly hostile to a host of institutions: the judiciary, the Bank of England, the Treasury, the Office for Budget Responsibility and indeed parliament itself have all been attacked implicitly or explicitly by Conservative prime ministers since 2016, undermining the institutional stability that is an essential pre-requisite for strong economic growth. As the UK looks ahead to more economic disruption from big structural shifts such as an ageing population, climate change and automation, the Conservatives must return the concept of stewardship to the heart of its economic approach.

One Nation

The third abiding principle is that of One Nation. The left often tries to caricature Conservatism as a heartless ideology, which prioritises the interests of the richest in society at the expense of those less well off. The truth, however, is that a belief in the need for economic prosperity to be shared across society has been a consistent theme of Conservatism. It is a concern most strongly associated with Disraeli, who worried about there being 'Two nations; between whom there is no intercourse and no sympathy . . . and [who] are not governed by the same laws: the rich and the poor.'[5] It is a principle that has recurred consistently, however: Peel's Corn Law reforms were aimed at helping the least well off at the expense of the most; while in the post-war years Harold Macmillan argued that the Conservative Party had 'a clear duty to those sections of people who have not shared in this general prosperity'. This principle stems in part from the desire for stability discussed above and in part by the belief that everyone should have an equal opportunity to achieve their potential, regardless of their background – both of which are undermined by high levels of economic inequality. At its best, therefore, Conservatism has balanced the desire for broad-based prosperity with the need to foster aspiration. But, by failing to do more to address the sharp rise in economic inequality the UK has witnessed since the 1980s, the Conservative Party has not lived up to the One Nation principle in recent years. With structural factors likely to continue to put upward pressure on economic inequality, this must be put right.

This belief in One Nation is distinct from concerns about the distribution more usually associated with Labour. One Nation is a unifying principle based on finding common ground between different sections of society rather than fostering the politics of envy. By contrast, the left has consistently pursued the politics of class war, sowing division and a sense of grievance, and arguing that many of society's challenges could be solved if only a small number of the very richest could be made to pay their fair share.

Empowerment

The final enduring Conservative principle pertains to the role of the state. Conservatives have been profoundly sceptical about the type of controlling and interventionist state that has become associated with the economics of the left during the twentieth century. The bar for state intervention must be high: as Nigel Lawson put it, 'for intervention to be justified, it must be demonstrated that the imperfections of government action are less serious than the imperfection of the market that the intervention in question is intended to correct. And this is not an easy condition to satisfy.'[6]

But having spent the previous century defining itself against *laissez-faire* liberalism, Conservatism has never been libertarianism. As Thatcher said, 'we are not anti-State. On the contrary, we seek a proper balance between State and society.'[7] Rather, the Conservative concept of the state has consistently seen its role as an enabler, rather than controller, of economic activity. This has meant different things over time: Disraeli's social reforms in the nineteenth century; pursuing a programme of state-led economic rationalisation of industry in the 1920s to try to restore competitiveness; the adoption of the welfare state in the post-war period; and, of course, the state's rollback under Thatcher. But, even at its most interventionist under Macmillan, the pitch was nevertheless about reducing control, cutting taxes, reducing spending and unlocking private sector investment. It was not, as the late historian of Conservative thinking E.H.H. Green put it, 'the welfare state mixed economy is safe in our hands'.[8]

This is the principle from which perhaps the Conservatives seem to have departed least in recent years; particularly given the Labour Party's shift towards widespread government control under Jeremy Corbyn; this made the Conservatives look like the continued champion of a more balanced role for the state. But the enormous expansion of the state ushered in by

Covid and the energy fallout from Russia's invasion of Ukraine, while in themselves justifiable, risk setting a precedent that government intervention is the default response to any economic challenge. Conservatism must resist this, staying true to the principle that the state's role is to empower rather than control economic activity.

The UK economy's challenges

These four principles – pragmatism, stewardship, One Nation and empowerment – emerge as consistent themes from the last two centuries of Conservative economics. The task for modern Conservatives is to apply them to the contemporary economic challenges facing the UK. There are three that must be addressed above all.

The first is growth. On a GDP per capita basis, the UK economy grew by just seven per cent between 2007 and 2022, and labour productivity by just four per cent.[9] These figures feed into a grim picture for living standards, with real wages currently not expected to return to their 2008 level until 2027.[10] This all compares miserably with the UK's experience of strong economic and productivity growth in the more than half century between the end of the Second World War and the global financial crisis.

Delivering higher economic and productivity growth is essential for improving living standards and generating opportunity. The good news is that there is reason to believe that the right policy package can make a material difference. On the eve of Covid, the UK's productivity was seventeen per cent lower than the average of France, Germany and the United States.[11] The success of the Thatcher era supply side reforms in closing a previous gap, which culminated in the decades leading up to the financial crisis seeing UK income per head growing faster than those countries, should give us confidence that ambitious economic reform can once again do the same.[12]

Yet, while the stewardship principle means that Conservativism understands the need for change and reform to drive progress, Conservatism's inherent pragmatism means it is also realistic. The UK's growth and productivity travails over the last fifteen years are not simply or even mainly the result of policy failure. For a start, the UK has suffered four massive economic shocks, all of which have done permanent damage to the economy. While it is true that the economic hit from the type of Brexit pursued results directly from UK government policy, the other three shocks – the financial crisis, Covid and the fallout from the war in Ukraine – cannot be laid primarily at the door of UK government policy.

Furthermore, while the slowdown since 2008 has undoubtedly been pronounced, it is simply an exacerbation of an existing trend. UK GDP per capita growth had already been slowing gradually for decades even before the financial crisis, averaging 2.5 per cent in the 1980s, 1.9 per cent in the 1990s, 1.2 per cent in the 2000s and 1.1 per cent in the 2010s.[13] The same is true of productivity: taken on a ten-year rolling average, labour productivity slowed steadily from around 3.5 per cent a year in the mid-1970s to around 1.5 per cent before the financial crisis.[14]

This slowdown is common across advanced economies, which strongly suggests structural forces are at play. A big part of the story stems from demographics: advanced economies experienced a huge growth and productivity tailwind in the second half of the twentieth century as the baby boomer generation not only entered the workforce, but did so with much higher levels of education than their predecessors. That headwind is now turning into a tailwind as the baby boomers retire, shrinking the working-age proportion of the population, while the one-off boost to educational performance has faded. Alongside this, the gradual but inevitable shift of economies out of higher productivity goods into lower productivity services as they grow richer has increasingly weighed on productivity.[15]

Looking ahead, these forces will almost certainly continue to weigh on growth. And, while some economists argue that technological advances in areas like artificial intelligence hold out the prospect of transforming productivity,[16] others, such as Robert Gordon, believe that technological innovation is in fact slowing.[17] All this means that while policy can undoubtedly make a difference, Conservatives should treat with deep scepticism those on both left and right, arguing that our economic prospects can be so transformed as to restore economic and productivity growth to the levels seen in the second half of the twentieth century. So, while a bold agenda to improve the UK's economic performance is needed, Conservative economics, grounded in pragmatism, must not use the pursuit of growth as an excuse to ignore the other two long-term challenges facing the UK: high levels of inequality and an unsustainable fiscal position.

Since the 1980s, economic inequality has risen sharply in the UK, to hit levels that are high by both historic and international standards. Measured by the Gini coefficient, income inequality has risen from 26.7 in 1980 to 34.4 in 2020/21, while the share of income going to the top one per cent has gone from 6.8 per cent to twelve per cent.[18] This means the UK has one of the highest levels of income inequality in the OECD.[19] Regional inequality has also risen over the last forty years, as London and the south east have pulled away from other parts of the country;[20] and, while inequalities of wealth have increased less sharply, they have nevertheless risen and remain high, with the wealth held by the top one per cent of households greater than for the bottom 80 per cent combined.[21]

Again, structural factors are at play. Across advanced economies technology has driven a hollowing out of middle-income jobs and increased demand for high-skilled workers, while globalisation has reduced the demand for low and middle-income jobs. But policy has also made a difference: the weakening of trade unions and cuts to working-age welfare have both contributed to higher inequality, for example; while significant rises in the national minimum wage have acted in the opposite direction.

There are some on the right who play into the stereotype that Conservatives should not care about inequality: as Chancellor, Kwasi Kwarteng said that 'for too long in this country, we have indulged in a fight over redistribution. Now, we need to focus on growth.'[22] But Conservatism properly grounded in the principles of One Nation and stewardship should absolutely see high levels of economic inequality as a problem: they undermine political and economic stability, opening the door to populists; they act to limit social mobility, undermining the pursuit of equality of opportunity that all Conservatives claim they support; and there is no evidence that higher inequality is needed to deliver higher growth.[23]

The third structural challenge is managing long-term pressures on the public finances. The last fifteen years have seen the UK's fiscal position take a battering, with national debt nearly tripling as a share of GDP to around 100 per cent of GDP, the highest level since the 1950s.[24] In the years following the financial crisis, rock-bottom borrowing costs led economists to become more relaxed about high levels of government debt. But the recent sharp rise in interest rates across advanced economies has led to steeply rising debt servicing costs, while the fallout from the Truss–Kwarteng mini-budget in September 2022 was a reminder that bond markets continue to be a real constraint on governments' ability to borrow.

Looking forward, the fiscal picture will remain highly challenging, driven by some of those same structural factors that will weigh on growth, particularly our ageing population, as well as health spending coming under increasing pressure from technological improvements and a higher frequency of chronic health conditions. Over the next half century, the

Office for Budget Responsibility (OBR) projects that government spending on health, state pensions and adult social care
will rise from around fifteen per cent of GDP to 25 per cent.[25]
As a result, the UK's debt-to-GDP ratio is projected to rise
rapidly on an unsustainable path to around 250 per cent in
fifty years' time.[26] In order to counter these trends, the OBR
projects fiscal policy will need to be tightened each decade by
about £37 billion a year in today's terms.[27]

No Conservative should be comfortable with this. Liz
Truss's obsession with the tax burden above the need for sound
public finances was a repudiation of over two hundred years
of Conservative economics: from William Pitt's temporary
introduction of income tax, made permanent by Robert Peel;
Austen Chamberlain's Excess Profits Tax to pay for the cost
of the First World War; Geoffrey Howe's infamous tax-raising
budget of 1981; to the more recent tax rises of George Osborne
and Rishi Sunak, Conservatives have always prioritised sound
money over low taxes. It must continue do so.

Renewed Conservative economics in practice

The growth challenge, the inequality challenge and the fiscal
challenge: these are the challenges Conservative economics
must tackle in the coming decades, grounded in the enduring principles set out above: pragmatism; stewardship; One
Nation; and empowerment.

This chapter will close by discussing what this approach
might mean for policy in practice, looking at the main economic levers the government has at its disposal: macro; supply
side; and tax and social security. This should not be read as
an encyclopaedic policy manifesto, but rather a flavour of the
priorities and direction of travel required.

Macro-economic framework

The starting point must be a coherent macro-economic framework, which has a vital underpinning role to play in tackling all three challenges set out above.

The UK's macro framework has historically had strong international credibility, based on an independent Bank of England setting monetary policy combined with fiscal policy framed by rules set by the Treasury and independent forecasts from the OBR. The crisis that followed the 2022 mini-budget served as a stark reminder that such credibility cannot be taken for granted. The market meltdown was of course driven in significant part by the unsustainable fiscal stance, but it also resulted in part from the sustained attack that this institutional framework came under from Truss and her team, including question marks raised during the leadership campaign over the Bank of England's independence; the sacking of Treasury Permanent Secretary Tom Scholar; and the refusal to publish an OBR forecast alongside the mini-budget. All of this served to undermine the UK's institutional credibility and contributed to a specific risk premium being attached to UK government bonds. This recklessness was profoundly un-Conservative, given how central institutions have been to the principle of stewardship. Reaffirming Conservatism's belief in the importance of the UK's macro institutional framework, and indeed looking to strengthen it, must be an essential building block to any coherent Conservative economic approach.

Looking specifically at the operation of fiscal policy, three objectives must be juggled: managing economic shocks; ensuring the sustainability of the public finances; and supporting long-term growth. Given the trade-offs between these objectives, a pragmatic approach is required. In terms of responding to shocks, fiscal policy should be willing to act aggressively in downturns to support the economy as a whole and the most vulnerable specifically, particularly when monetary policy is constrained as it was going into Covid. But when monetary is not at the zero lower bound, while fiscal policy must continue to protect the most vulnerable, it should primarily be monetary policy's role to manage the economic cycle. This is particularly true when a downturn coincides with an inflationary shock, as following Russia's invasion of Ukraine. While targeted support to protect the most vulnerable will often still be necessary, broad-based fiscal support simply risks making inflation worse.

The quid pro quo of being willing to use fiscal policy aggressively during downturns is that the job of fixing the public finances when the economy is growing must also be more aggressive. If good economic times are not used to get the debt-to-GDP ratio down materially, it will simply ratchet up over time with each economic shock, leaving the UK ever more exposed to the risk of higher and higher debt servicing costs. Given the long-term pressures discussed above, this will require some politically unpalatable decisions. On the spending side, for example, as the population ages it is simply unsustainable for the state pension to continue to rise in line with the triple lock. Further, the current debate around public services obsesses about how much is spent rather than the outcomes produced. The UK's improved educational performance in recent years serves as a reminder that public service reform can deliver better outcomes even within a constrained spending environment. A renewed focus on public services reform and efficiency is therefore essential. Yet, given the sheer scale of the spending pressures facing the state from population ageing and rising healthcare costs in particular, it is simply unrealistic to expect the same level of public service provision without spending rising further as a share of GDP. That means Conservatism needs to be honest about the fact that the tax burden will also need to rise, albeit gradually and moderately.

Alongside managing shocks and ensuring sustainable public finances, fiscal policy should prioritise targeted interventions – of both tax and spending – to support the economic growth. By failing to distinguish between the investment spending essential for growth and day-to-day spending, the Conservatives' current fiscal rules do not do so. This should be rectified, moving back to a situation where day-to-day spending is fully funded, while allowing borrowing for investment purposes, though with flexibility in the interpretation of these rules to ensure investment in human capital is not de-prioritised, something that has contributed to the UK's historic under-investment in this area.

Supply side reform

Providing fiscal support for long-term growth is an important underpinning of the second area Conservatives should prioritise, that of supply side reform. While the Truss administration's fiscal stance was deeply un-Conservative, its desire to focus on the supply side was right, essential as it is to increasing trend growth. At the heart of a Conservative approach should be the principle of government providing the enabling conditions to empower the private sector to deliver growth. Conservatism is not libertarianism: it should acknowledge the need for the government to intervene to correct market failure and be clear that a strategic approach to industrial policy is required. But it should also reject the idea promulgated on the left that the answer to every economic problem requires yet more tinkering by the state. There should be a high bar for government intervention, with Conservatism being as realistic about the risk of government failure as it is about the need to correct market failure. Within that overall framework, two areas of supply side reform should be prioritised: the provision of public goods and delivering the right competition and regulatory regime.

Because they provide positive spillovers, public goods – particularly infrastructure, innovation and skills – will typically be under-funded if left to the private sector. The government will also have to provide a co-ordinating role to ensure that the public and private sectors are aligned. As discussed above, a pragmatic trade-off must be made with the fiscal challenge, but spending in public goods should be prioritised. This is something that recent Conservative governments have got right in relation to infrastructure and innovation, with the May and Johnson administrations raising capital spending to its highest sustained level since the 1970s,[28] alongside putting in place a robust institutional framework to focus on delivery, from the UK Infrastructure Bank and the National Infrastructure Commission to the Advanced Research and Invention Agency (ARIA). Going forward, the same level of ambition needs to be shown when it comes to skills. The UK labour force will need to adapt to the long-term impacts of Covid, Brexit, rising geopolitical tensions and, most significantly, automation. To ensure it is prepared, the UK must show the same level of ambition when it comes to investing in human capital as it does in physical capital.

Alongside investment in public goods, the UK needs a pro-growth competition and regulatory regime. Competition policy can help tackle both the growth and inequality challenges, driving up productivity, while lowering prices for consumers. But there are worrying signs that competition has been weakening in the UK, with measures of competition such as profitability, concentration and firm entry and exit lessening in recent years.[29] The UK's competition regime should be strengthened, giving the Competition and Markets Authority stronger powers to protect consumers and tackle anti-competitive behaviour, along with expanding its duties to promote innovation and growth.

When it comes to the UK's future regulatory regime, the obsession with cutting red tape on parts of the right needs to be replaced with a more strategic conversation about making the UK a leader in the regulation of new growth areas such as artificial intelligence, robotics and cutting-edge healthcare.

Alongside this, Conservative economics must finally commit to reforming the UK's planning system, which acts as a major drag on growth: it holds back delivery of much-needed infrastructure, while the high property prices that result divert investment away from more efficient uses, reducing labour market mobility and raising barriers to entry for new businesses. It also entrenches inequality by artificially tilting the benefits of growth towards property owners. The politics are nightmarish but it is an area that must be prioritised.

Tax and social security

Along with planning, the other area of reform which is likely to require the most expenditure of political capital is in relation to tax.

Liz Truss was right: the UK has a tax problem that is holding back growth. That problem is not, however, the overall tax burden. It is true that the tax burden is on course to rise to its highest level since the Second World War as the country faces up to the structural pressures driving the fiscal challenge discussed above. But perspective is required: the UK's tax burden in 2020 remained below the OECD average,[30] and there is no clear link between a country's overall tax burden and its growth or productivity performance. Instead, the focus should be on reform. The UK tax system is riddled with unfair and economically damaging inefficiencies and anomalies. Drawing upon the One Nation and empowerment principles in particular, tax reform can play a vital part in tackling all three challenges identified above: redistributing more to help reduce inequality; improving incentives to boost growth; and ensuring sufficient revenues are raised to tackle the fiscal challenge.

There is no shortage of candidates for a renewed Conservative agenda of tax reform. The existing taxation of earnings is unfair and inefficient, allowing people to pay vastly different rates of tax for the same type of work depending on how they structure their tax affairs. The business tax system is full of badly targeted reliefs, while failing adequately to incentivise the investment that is so desperately needed. The UK's system of property taxation tax is a mess, with high levels of stamp duty disincentivising transactions, leading to a poor allocation of housing stock and reducing labour market flexibility, accompanied by a regressive annual property tax in the form of council tax. And inheritance tax is so full of reliefs and exemptions that it allows the richest to pay significantly lower rates than those much less well off: the effective rate paid on estates between £2 and 3 million is twice that on estates worth over £10 million.[31]

Tax reform inevitably creates losers, requiring the expenditure of political capital, and raising revenue is a task no Tory Chancellor revels in. But Geoffrey Howe serves as an example of a Chancellor who did both successfully, raising significant revenue when needed in his famous 1981 Budget, while also fundamentally restructuring the system away from the taxation of earnings towards consumption taxes. A true Thatcherite Conservative would have the reform of the tax system – rather than an obsession about its overall burden – at the heart of their economic strategy. Tax reform must be accompanied by social security reform. The welfare system should incentivize people into the labour market, in line with the empowerment principle, and ensure there is a sufficient safety net to support people through economic shocks and disruption, in line with the stewardship principle. At the moment, it does neither as well as it should.

While the system of Universal Credit performed admirably during Covid – a reminder of a successful recent Conservative economic reform – the fact that it needed to be topped up by £20 a week shone a light on the fact that the existing safety net was insufficient to deal with significant shocks. This stems from the UK having one of the least generous levels of unemployment benefit in the OECD, which is at its lowest in three decades and leaves UK workers less financially resilient to deal with economic shocks.[32] This relative lack of generosity is linked to the contributory principle that William Beveridge put at the heart of his vision for the welfare state being almost entirely missing from the current system. The contributory principle should be reintroduced, with people who have paid into the system while in work receiving, for a time-limited period, higher basic levels of support when they are out of work. This will ensure they have a bigger safety net to fall back on in hard times, and give them the time to find a job that most suits their skills, or undertake retraining, which will bring wider economic benefits. By time limiting the uplift, however, it will also ensure that the incentive to go back into the work-force remains.

Incentives should then be improved in other areas of the system. The marginal effective tax rate for someone on Universal Credit remains much higher than the tax rates facing top earners, so the case remains for reducing the taper rate at which benefits are withdrawn as people move into work. Ideally, these should be targeted at second-earner households where the disincentive to work remains the highest.

Above all, the Conservatives must move on from the divisive rhetoric that frames the debate between those who are willing to work hard and do the right thing, and those who choose to be on welfare. Instead, the social security system should reflect core Conservative principles: stewarding people through economic shocks, while ensuring people are incentivized to find work in line with the empowerment principle.

Conclusion

The above policy proposals serve as practical examples of the type of approach that a renewed framework for Conservative economics needs to take. The key point, however, is that

Conservative economics has got lost in recent years, increasingly refusing to engage in the trade-offs inherent in economic policymaking, while ignoring a rich history of Conservative economic thought. Above all, therefore, it needs to re-find its roots and get real about the challenges that lie ahead. That means moving on from half-baked versions of Thatcherism to embrace once again the historic Conservative principles of pragmatism, stewardship, One Nation and empowerment, and applying those to the big structural challenges facing the UK economy: increasing trend growth, reducing high levels of economic inequality and managing huge long-term pressures on the public finances.

All this will require a confrontation of trade-offs and a willingness to be unpopular in the short term to do what is in the long-term national interest. This used to be the essence of Conservatism; the task is to ensure it becomes so once again.

6

Tackling the Health Crisis
Anne Milton

The challenges facing the centre right in the crucial and highly emotive area of health are formidable. Public satisfaction with the NHS is at an all-time low, patients are waiting too long for treatment after the delays caused by Covid shutdowns, and staff morale is crumbling. Add to this an ageing population, and the increasing expectations of a twenty-first-century electorate, and it is clear that a centre right government needs to develop an economically realistic, politically deliverable, and technologically cutting-edge approach to health improvement and care that works for everyone and can address these ongoing challenges.

The National Health Service was created, free at the point of use, in 1948. Within a year, resource constraints saw its architect, Aneurin Bevan, threatening to resign over proposed charges for prescriptions and, two years later, he finally went in protest at the introduction of charges for glasses and false teeth. Almost from the beginning the key challenge of running a wholly state-funded NHS was apparent: what happens when the demand exceeds what the taxpayer is prepared to pay? Seventy-five years later, we're still rubbing up against the same problem.

After training as a nurse I worked for 25 years in the NHS that Bevan created, before becoming Public Health Minister in the Coalition government. I saw at first hand the problems that we are still trying to resolve today: poor housing; hospital beds blocked by people ready to be discharged; illness caused by damaging lifestyles; and resistance of the NHS to change.

The Covid pandemic, and the government's response to it, shows that health threats can still be a serious danger to society, both directly in terms of health problems, but also economically. Political parties win elections not only if they are trusted with the economy and run it well, but if the public believes that they can trust that political party with the NHS. The trust of the public on the NHS can make or break a general election.

Keeping people well

The level of services the NHS needs to provide is clearly related to the health of the people. Of course, this is not the only driver, but it is an area where we know government intervention can make a difference, and indeed *has* made a difference on, for instance, smoking related diseases.

People who are well are happier, can earn and spend (increasing GDP and paying taxes), and need less healthcare, whether that be drugs for diabetes and depression or surgery for blocked arteries. It is estimated that around a half of all working days are lost due to stress, anxiety and depression – around seventeen to eighteen million each year. Economics is not the only argument for keeping people well, but a health service under pressure needs all the help it can get, and this we can do something about.

The room for improvement in population health is clear, as are the benefits of reducing health inequalities. The impact on your health of being rich or poor is stark. A woman in the most deprived areas of the country can expect to die nearly eight years younger than one in the least deprived areas, while for men the difference is nearly ten years. *Healthy* life expectancy at birth in the most deprived areas is over eighteen years less than in the least deprived areas.[1] Three-quarters of people aged 45 to 74 are obese or overweight. But the rate in the most deprived areas is fourteen percentage points higher than in the least deprived.[2] These shocking figures on inequality have so far failed to push any government into significant action.

That change *can* be achieved is shown by significant falls in smoking rates, for example. This was in part due to government intervention to ban smoking in public places, but the legislation had an impact beyond that envisaged; it has brought about a wider cultural change, which has reduced domestic smoking habits as well. However, a quarter of those on lower incomes still smoke, as against ten per cent of those on higher incomes. Mental health shows similar disparities with around sixteen per cent of adults reporting moderate to severe depression, with those in more deprived areas twice as likely to have symptoms; mental health problems are a major cause of inability to work.

The cost of living well into old age matters not just because of the costs of social and NHS care but in economic inactivity. There is major potential for improving the nation's health, with the useful side effect of boosting the economy and reducing pressure on health services. However, despite overall improvements in health over the last century, these health inequalities show a worrying trend. In a follow-up to his government-commissioned 2008 report Professor Sir Michael Marmot stated in 2018:[3] '. . . in England, health is getting worse for people living in more deprived districts and regions, health inequalities are increasing and, for the population as a whole, health is declining'.

The politics of improving health

There are difficulties for a party of the right in addressing these issues. Those of us who believe in individual liberty and personal responsibility are naturally averse to restricting people's freedom to decide for themselves what they eat, what they drink, and what they spend their money on. To be fair, it is not only Conservatives who have a problem. The Blair government had a difficult time over the legislation to ban smoking in public places, with some Labour MPs believing that it would make the lives of those on lower incomes more miserable, and thus alienate their core vote. And, it has to be said, both parties can sometimes appear to be strongly influenced by the vested interests of producers of products that harm health. Nonetheless, the case for government action has now become compelling. Despite the links between lifestyle and poor health, no government has shown sufficient leadership on improving the public's health.

Our bodies are programmed by genetics to eat well in times of plenty, but most of us can afford far more calories (and salt, and sugar) than we need every day. Modern advertising is very powerful in directing us to what people want to sell us, and the ordinary consumer has only the barest information about the ingredients in most of the processed food we eat. The evidence that obesity, drinking above government guidelines, smoking and lack of exercise are causes of ill health is overwhelming. Added to this, ill health can have adverse consequences beyond the effects on the individual. For example, for the 1.4 million people who are addicted to gambling, debt and family breakdown often follow. The most deprived groups are often those with the least access to information and the least ability to make choices.

There is a clear role for government in balancing the information available to consumers and, sometimes in direct legislative action; who now would advocate the return of smoking in restaurants? The Cameron soft drinks industry levy, the so-called sugar tax, has also had an impact. The total sugar sold in soft drinks between 2015 and 2019 decreased by 35.4 per cent from 135,000 tonnes to 87,000 tonnes.

While it is early days to suggest causality, early reports suggest that there has been a drop in obesity among primary-aged children. Similarly early reports of the impact of minimum unit pricing of alcohol in Scotland show a reduction in alcohol sales and a positive impact at population level. The evidence is clear that government action to improve health, particularly for those whose health is poorest, would reduce costs to the NHS, enable more people of working age to work, help people remain well in retirement, and improve GDP. With the CBI estimating that health-related economic inactivity is costing the UK £180bn a year, the case for action is not a difficult one.

Getting rid of siloed government and the dead hand of Whitehall

Government policies on health, housing, planning, the environment, benefits and education all affect health outcomes. As an example, for a population in good health we need to give children the best start in life, educate them, equip them to get a good job, and ensure that they have access to open spaces and good leisure opportunities. But each department acts in its own silo, developing policy without formal consideration of its health effects. There is currently very limited input about the potential impacts that policies across government have on health, and one reason for this is that nearly all of the bandwidth of the Department of Health is taken up in dealing with the NHS.

Amid the storm of Andrew Lansley's 2012 Health and Social Care Act, it went somewhat unnoticed that responsibility for public health had returned to local authority control for the first time since 1974. The change reflected the fact that improvements to public health depend more on environment, education, income and well-being than they do on the NHS. Local authorities have some powers to influence all these areas, but the British tendency to centralise everything means that Whitehall still holds many of the levers, including the purse-strings. In particular, moving money between NHS and other local budgets is difficult. The Cameron government experimented with increasing devolution to Metropolitan authorities, with some success; developing this on larger scale would enable health improvement activity to be much better targeted to local needs.

There is a strong case that the centre right should make for creating a ministerial post with a cross-government remit for promoting health through policy in all government departments (the existing post of Minister for Women and Equalities provides a model). This would help a wider understanding across government of the impact of poor health on the economy. Alongside this, making a formal Health Impact Assessment an obligatory part of all government policy development would go some way towards alerting ministers to the fact that the policy they develop could contribute to, or may harm, the efforts to improve the wider determinants of health. Conservatives believe strongly in policies that boost the economy. So, keeping people in work, and keeping people able to continue to earn when they are older through improved health is something we should seize. If implemented effectively both of these would be a strong signal of a step change in Conservative thinking; a shift from the *laissez-faire* right towards the caring centre.

Levelling up may have started as just a slogan, but it is necessary if the country is to prosper, and health cannot be excluded from it. It's not just transport links and business investment that are needed in more deprived regions, but people healthy enough to work. A Conservative government must act nationally where legislation is needed, but also devolve both powers and funding to local authorities, to enable them to address the wider determinants of health through approaches targeted on local needs.

Living with economic reality

While the NHS can never fully meet demand, the service is currently falling well below what is acceptable to the public. Can we afford to keep a state-funded NHS model, maintain its growth at or around the same proportion of GDP and increase efficiency to get more people treated and cared for per pound spent?

Demand for healthcare, if not actually infinite has, since the formation of the NHS, always exceeded the resources available. Waiting lists, A&E queues, and pressure to introduce new drugs and treatments have been present since the beginning, and there is certainly no indication that the demand will slow: with rapid advances in life sciences but a stone's throw away from being able to predict disease years in advance; preventative drug treatments in development; swifter interventions when disease strikes; people living longer but with long-term illness and decreased mobility; and the belief that healthcare will ever more speedily make us better or prolong our lives. Public expectations have grown and will continue to grow.

Set against this have been remarkable innovations that have increased the efficiency of the service. Short-stay surgery, endoscopy, new understanding of disease, and new drugs all mean that healthcare systems now treat far more patients than in the past in far fewer hospital beds. There is no reason to believe we have reached the limits of this efficiency, so long as the system is able to innovate and change the way it works.

UK total healthcare spending remained at around ten per cent of GDP from 2009 until the 'Covid jump' in 2020.[4] This is lower than France and Germany (11–12%), about the same as The Netherlands, and higher than Italy, Spain or Australia (8.5–9.5%).[5] This is total spending (private and government); of this, 80 per cent was government spending, representing about eighteen per cent of total government spending in 2019–2020.[6]

Upward pressure on this expenditure is anticipated due to the increasing proportion of older people compared with those working, to technological developments, and to increasing levels of obesity and other health risks. New improved drugs and techniques are, in the main, desirable, and we need to plan to incorporate these. Ageing is inevitable, but need not necessarily result in more ill health; improving the health of older as well as younger people will make health services more affordable.

Since 1982, UK healthcare spending has risen on average 4.1 per cent per year, against growth in GDP of just over two per cent over the same period. Given the multiple other pressures on government, it would be unrealistic to plan for a significant increase in government contribution to healthcare over and above GDP growth (other than perhaps temporarily to reverse the lockdown-related increases in waiting lists). So, keeping health services affordable will need, at the least, continued economic growth and success in reducing the burden of illness in both the young and the old. If these are insufficient, or cannot be achieved, then we will need more tax spending, or an increase in the proportion of funding from non-government sources.

Enabling access for all to world-class healthcare

Conservatives remain committed to the principle that healthcare of the highest standards should be available to all when they need it, regardless of their ability to pay. This is the norm for all developed countries (except the USA), and the

British people deserve no less. Any debate is only about how this can be organised – both in funding and provision.

Paying for services

So how should the UK fund population-wide access to the NHS and related health services? Three models of healthcare funding are visible in western Europe and North America today. The first is the one we already have in place – the tax-funded system seen in the UK and most of Scandinavia. Government decides how much of the tax take should be spent on healthcare and distributes this to pay for services. Some measure of local decision-making is usually involved (integrated care boards in England, local authorities in Scandinavia). The model has the advantages of a universal easily understood entitlement, low revenue-collection costs, and good cost-control as government is the dominant buyer of services. However, it means healthcare is in constant competition with other government priorities for resources, and national politicians (at least in the UK) are seen as responsible for, and blamed for, any deficiency.

Secondly, there is the 'Bismarckian' social insurance model of Germany, France, and many other European states. Employers and individuals pay an identifiable health insurance premium, either to the state or a private insurer, usually with a measure of compulsion. The state funds the unemployed and those otherwise unable to pay, and entitlement to care when sick is essentially universal. The system benefits from having identifiable contributions largely ring-fencing health from other government priorities, and facilitates topping-up contributions to buy additional services, but can be vulnerable to changes in income in economic downturns, and has to include the costs of revenue collection if private insurers are used.

Finally, there is the American system of private insurance with government meeting the costs of the poor and elderly.

While this allows individuals (or their employers) to buy the level/quality of healthcare they can afford, it leaves the working-age uninsured without affordable care, and cost-control is very poor. In addition, government inevitably gets drawn in to cover the poor and elderly, with the result that the US spends more government money (8.5 per cent GDP in 2019) on healthcare than does the UK (8.1 per cent GDP in 2019).[7]

Despite calls, mainly from the political right, for the UK to move to a social insurance model, there are no clear net advantages to doing this. The state would still have to underwrite a large part of the cost (as all European governments and the US government do); it would introduce a third party (insurers) into the process with consequent increase in costs and no significant benefit; and it would be an immense political challenge.

Despite its current woes, the NHS remains among the best-loved and most respected of British institutions. Although generally sceptical of 'big government', Conservatives, and the British people, recognise that one purpose of government is to enable us to act collectively in areas where individual action is not practicable. The hugely uneven distribution of the misfortunes of ill health are clearly one such area, and tax-funded health services symbolise the settled will of the British people to share the burdens of such misfortune together.

That is not to say, though, that there is no place for health insurance and individual voluntary contributions as a way to relieve pressure on the NHS if people wish to use them. The important principle is simply that the tax-funded service should be available, at high quality, to all. A system in which people could use private funding to 'top-up' their NHS entitlement to care, may be worth considering, and has the potential to bring more money into the healthcare system without increasing taxes. Australia has had this type of arrangement for many years with health outcomes similar to, or better than, the UK, and without the state-funded sector collapsing into the type of inadequate rump that the left would predict. This model needs the NHS to use the National Tariff Payment System as a baseline price to allow a range of providers to enter the market, providing services either at that rate or more expensively, topped up where necessary from patients' own resources (insured or out-of-pocket). This would raise predictable howls of fury from the left, as it did when the Blair government skated close to this under Alan Milburn and John Reid in the early 2000s, but the Australian experience suggests the predicted collapse of the NHS is unlikely to happen. This has the potential to take some of the load from the NHS, without damaging the universal service.

Providing the service

Since the start of the NHS in 1948, service provision has been a mixed public/private partnership. Hospitals were nationalised, while general practices were left as private enterprises funded by the state, and nursing/care-home provision was in the hands of local authorities and private businesses or charities. Private hospital provision was essentially confined to private beds in NHS hospitals but, over the subsequent decades, a substantial private hospital and care-home sector has emerged.

But the state is not always the best provider. Around the turn of the century the Major/Blair governments appeared to have reached a rough consensus that improving healthcare would involve NHS-funded commissioners arranging NHS care from a mix of semi-independent public providers and private providers. This was reflected in the Major government's 'internal market' and GP fundholding, and the Blair government's development of NHS foundation trusts. The intention was to improve both quality and efficiency by allowing innovation, and a measure of competition, within a regulated environment to underwrite standards. Some measure of local variation was implicit in this, as commissioners reflected local needs in their purchasing, and innovative providers tried out different models of care.

Later governments, Labour, Coalition and Conservative, progressively stepped back from this under pressure from vested interests (professional and trade union), ideology, and the political difficulties of defending the inevitable small variations that would result ('postcode lotteries'). The result is that we seem to be back where we were in the 1980s, with increasing cries for 'more money' to be poured into the same system, and the government impotently trying to direct improvements by Whitehall decree across the entire service.

Conservatives should welcome further expansion of a mixed economy of provision, and should allow the proper development of the original concept, squashed by Old Labour ideology and vested interests. This would allow the emergence of local competitors, spurring investment and innovation in both techniques and working practices, to the ultimate benefit of patients.

A related issue arises around NHS terms of service and working practices. Despite foundation trusts having always had the power to set local pay rates, etc, this has almost never been used on any scale, even though market wage rates and (for example) housing costs vary widely across the country. Why are hospitals not taking the opportunity to get more care for the taxpayers' £ by looking to local pay scales where this is possible? In this can be seen the unholy alliance of the Whitehall centralisers and national professional and trade-union interests keen to preserve power and influence, actively discouraging innovation in this area. This must change, and moving accountability for services away from London to local elected bodies would incentivise this.

New technologies

Today's healthcare would be unrecognisable to Aneurin Bevan. Day surgery, flexible endoscopy, CT scanning, and powerful new drugs are just some of the developments that have helped push life expectancy up by over twelve years since 1951, while the number of hospital beds has decreased from 480,000 to 141,000 since the start of the NHS.

Technological progress will continue, with new drugs, treatment methods, and investigations already in development, and the health system will need to be able to deploy these as they appear if it is to remain credible. Some assessment of cost-effectiveness, such as carried out by NICE, is appropriate, but we need to plan for the extra costs of being able to do things that were previously impossible, offset to some extent by being able to do some other things at less cost.

Many new technologies require up-front investment (in buildings, equipment, staff, IT) before they can begin to produce their benefits, which are often cost reductions. A business would borrow to provide the investment, or take money from operating surpluses, paying it back over the next few years from the economies made or new income generated. The state-owned hospital sector, working with government annual budgeting rules, is unable to do this. Hospitals need to rely on capital grants distributed to serve short-term political priorities, or limit investment to projects that can deliver a return within the financial year. This is not a recipe for the efficient and rapid introduction of new health-improving or efficiency-generating technologies.

We need to free NHS Trusts to borrow for development (which was planned to be one of their freedoms originally, but squashed by Gordon Brown's Treasury), and in addition signal to private providers that investments they make will have the NHS as one of their potential customers. This does raise some questions of financial accountability, as the debts of

NHS Trusts would ultimately fall to the taxpayer to cover, but this is already the case for other public bodies (notably local authorities) and mechanisms similar to those already established could be put in place to mitigate the risks.

Caring for the elderly

An ageing population is increasing the dependency ratio (the number of non-working adults supported by people of working age). The future costs of this will depend to a significant extent on whether we become 'well' or 'unwell' older people. There are large gains to be made if we can stay well into our seventies, eighties and even nineties, but this will require a shift in how we look at old age. To push the age at which we need care upwards i.e. later in our lives, we need to make improving health an integral part of all government departments, rather than the poor relation in a Department of Health whose priority of focus is managing the NHS.

Paying for personal social care

However hard we try to keep well, there will come for many of us a time when we can no longer care for ourselves and need the help of others either in our homes or in residential care. At present, much of this care falls outside the NHS and is funded from a mixture of individual and local council payment in a system whose origins pre-date the NHS (about 35 per cent of care-home residents are self-funding, varying from about 50 per cent in the least-deprived areas to twenty per cent in the most-deprived). The injustices and inequities of this have been well rehearsed; the burden falls only on those unlucky enough to need this care, in contrast to the principles of the NHS where we all share the costs of those unlucky enough to be ill.

And those who have 'scrimped and saved all their lives' regret seeing the hoped-for inheritance of their children disappear, while those with small or no assets are funded by the state. A range of reports and commissions (most recently the David Cameron commissioned Dilnot Report (2011)) have rehearsed the problems and solutions to this, which essentially revolve around what balance of individual and government funding is fair and achievable. However, political follow-through has been in short supply. Theresa May's proposals probably contributed to her losing her majority in the 2017 election and the current government's reforms, due to come into effect in 2023, have been pushed back to 2025, with an election between now and then. The political bandwidth has never lasted long enough, and the political capital never been worth the risk to deliver the necessary change. The high costs of social care, which often have to be met from individual life savings or capital in their home, and the equity of who pays and for what, have not been grasped.

It is time to grasp this nettle. No policy is going to solve all the inequities, but the current government proposals (cap on lifetime care costs of £86,000 and only those with assets over £100,000 pay full costs) improve on the current system and have been assessed as affordable. This needs to be implemented by 2025 as planned, or earlier if possible. We have sat on this long enough; the time for action is now.

Bed blocking

Alongside the question of 'who pays?' for social care is the related issue of patients unable to be discharged from NHS beds because of a lack of social care. In part this is about the availability of paid carers, but funding also plays a part; the ability to transfer some of the cost of very expensive NHS beds to pay for social care is difficult when one is funded from Whitehall through the NHS and the other through local authorities. This problem is as old as the NHS itself.

Separate budgets will always stand in the way. Multiple attempts over decades to enable health and social care to work together to improve flows of patients haven't worked. Devolution of healthcare budgets to those who fund social care will mean the responsibility and authority rest within the same organisation. Despite social care being a block in the flow of healthcare, since 2010 the Conservative Party has only skated around the edge of budgetary devolution as a solution. The centre right should be proactive in making what we have work better through wholehearted devolution of health budgets.

Devolving decision-making

The NHS is overcentralised and, as a result, slow to react to local needs and subject to repeated changes of priorities as Westminster political fashions change. Bevan might have been keen that 'The sound of a dropped bedpan in Tredegar Hospital will reverberate round the Palace of Westminster', but it's no way to run a twenty-first-century health service. The Health Secretary and the ministers in Whitehall grapple to find ways of exercising control through frameworks and diktats, but this tends to result in the stifling of local innovation, while leaving the centre to be blamed for any shortcomings in the system.

Clearly, in a tax-funded system there needs to be political accountability for the service, but having this solely at Westminster inhibits the development of local priorities to meet local needs. It also means that all the heat from NHS criticism lands on the Secretary of State, much of it for things they can do very little about.

The Cameron/Osborne government embraced the idea of devolution (considering in the early years place-based budgets for all public services), and the Mayors of Combined

Authorities have grasped with enthusiasm the opportunity it brings to their local areas. They have now become significant political figures. Seen as an independent voice for their area rather than the political voice of their party, they have a voice that is often more influential than the local MPs and offer a real challenge to government. Critically they know their own areas in a way that Whitehall never can.

Commissioning of local health services is now under the control of Integrated Care Boards, accountable to NHS England and ultimately to the Secretary of State for Health. These boards are intended to work closely with elected local authorities, and others, to plan care. As it stands, this may be just a new version of the old Whitehall-directed model, with lip service paid to working with LAs. However, it holds the potential for developing proper, effective local control of health services. In Greater Manchester a combined authority (now the Greater Manchester ICP) took control of £6bn of NHS spending, and other local authorities are looking to get involved in similar initiatives. If government were to develop this into full devolution to local authorities it would enable commissioning of services to meet local needs, more fully integrate health and social care and, importantly, transfer much accountability from the Secretary of State to local councils and elected Mayors.

The centre right agenda for the health of our nation

The healthcare system in the UK is going to remain free at the point of use, funded from taxation, and available to all. There is no sensible economic case for changing this and, even if there were, it would be politically impossible. But to keep this afford-able at the standards to which the citizens of a rich economy are entitled, expect in the twenty-first century, that we need to make radical changes in how we keep people healthy, how we

provide care, and how and where we make the decisions about
the best way to spend what will always be constrained resources.
We need to implement a comprehensive programme of health
promotion, including regulatory changes, integrated across all
areas of government policy, with the objective of bringing the
health of all up to the levels enjoyed now by the most affluent,
and extending the period of healthy, active life as long as possible for everyone.

Secondly, we should devolve most healthcare funding and
commissioning decision-making to elected large local authorities to enable locally sensitive decision-making and flexibility,
including financial transfers between health and social care.
Along with this must be the implementation of the current government proposals for self-funding of social care as planned,
or sooner. We also need to return to the original concept of
foundation trusts able to set locally appropriate pay rates and
borrow for investment to enable rapid introduction of new
technologies and working practices. Alongside this should be
the development of a mixed public/private economy of providers to increase capacity, facilitate innovation, and improve
standards and efficiency through competition.

And, finally, the whole must be underpinned by wider
government economic policies, which will provide sufficient
GDP growth to enable the tax-funded NHS to absorb the cost
increases of new developments and an ageing population.
Should this prove inadequate, consideration needs to be given
to providing incentives, including through the tax system, to
encourage those who so wish to relieve the demands on the
NHS through private care, in whole or in part.

In summary, there exists an opportunity for the centre
right, guided like the British people by pragmatism rather than
ideology, to modernise Beveridge and Bevan's mid-twentieth-
century health and care model. Drawing on experience from
the UK and the rest of the world over the last three-quarters
of a century, concerted action to improve health, devolution of

decision-making to the lowest practicable level, and the development of more choice of provision will enable the tax-funded
model to continue to give an older (but healthier) population
the health and care they deserve through the twenty-first
century.

7

Winning the Global Race for Science and Technology
Sam Gyimah

Science, technology and innovation now cut across every aspect of government and our lives: from economic prosperity to health, through geopolitics, national security, and defence. Our recent experience with the Covid-19 pandemic exemplifies this and underscores the importance of world-changing innovation for our health and well-being; and our ability to tackle the big challenges of our time from climate change and an ageing population, to the future of how we live and work.

Furthermore, the global economy is shifting. Growth companies are fundamentally different today. They are characterised by intangible assets, are technologically driven, can scale and dominate individual markets very quickly, and require new forms of financing compared to the manufacturing-based economy of the past. In every sector, and across sectors, new technologies are transforming how the world operates. Quantum computing will give us superior computing power. Artificial intelligence will continue both to amaze and threaten us, with new applications and unexpected breakthroughs. Digitisation is putting every industry online. The energy transition away from fossil fuels and towards clean generation is already altering geopolitics.

Emerging technologies and the resources that underpin them can be leveraged for war, peace, or national prosperity. That is their strategic importance.

And to avoid the risk of losing key industries and to secure leadership positions of new battleground industries, rich countries and intergovernmental organisations are shifting to a 'new industrial strategy'; marshalling economic, scientific, defence and innovation policies to stay ahead of the game even at the risk of clashing with World Trade Organisation rules on 'protectionism'.

In the United States, for instance, the Biden administration passed the CHIPS and Science Act (August 2022), and the Inflation Reduction Act (August 2022) with hundreds of billions of subsidies; to position the US competitively, create jobs, improve productivity, strengthen supply chains, counter China, secure strategic autonomy, and enhance productivity – all based around the industries of the future.

In direct response to, and to compete with the Inflation Reduction Act, and the $369 billion of subsidies, in March 2023, the European Union announced the EU Net Zero Industry Act, with 'buy European' clauses to ensure new Green technologies are developed by European-based companies and to counter China.

In defence, NATO launched the first multi-sovereign, venture capital fund to invest $1 billion into emerging technologies that have dual use. As Jens Stoltenberg, NATO Secretary General, said at the launch of the innovation fund in July 2022: 'with a fifteen-year time frame, the NATO Innovation Fund will help to bring to life those nascent technologies that have the power to transform our security in the decades to come, strengthening the Alliance's innovation ecosystem and bolstering the security of our one billion citizens'.

China's 'Made in China 2025' state-led industrial policy aims to transform the country into a global leader in high-tech manufacturing, and is yet another example of how science and technology now cut across all aspects of policy.

A scramble to secure leadership positions is underway, fuelling protectionism, and in some cases pitting ally against ally, and making foes of would-be allies. Competing and winning in this global race is existential for Britain's prosperity and continued relevance in the world. Science, technology and innovation are now a material part of our everyday economy and everyday lives. And yet, as an island of almost seventy million people Britain cannot compete with the EU, US and China on its own. For post-Brexit Britain to be a master of its destiny it needs to rediscover the values of openness, fostering great institutions, pragmatism and a long-term approach to secure strategic dominance in the niche industries of the future, where it can best compete.

We cannot know the precise shape or structure of the future economy, but by appreciating and embracing economic and technological trends, we can make reasonable bets. A strategic state is one that can plan for the long term, match resources to its ambition, with a clear-eyed focus on what it takes to succeed being a necessary and sufficient condition for the country. Every country will have its own way of addressing these questions in terms of the role of the state, what works, and what level of intervention is necessary. But the strategic imperative is indisputable; and populist messages, which might make great bumper sticker campaign slogans but are devoid of policy content – such as 'Global Britain' and 'Levelling Up' – are not up to the task. Becoming a 'science superpower' is an arresting slogan, but success in modern scientific research is the result of years, sometimes decades, of painstaking international collaboration. A strategic state, not a populist one of the left or right, with the vision to transform the way we live, work and protect ourselves is what is required.

No more karaoke Thatcherism

A strong economy is the foundation stone of prosperity and security. And the transformational shift required is part of our national economic history. The Industrial Revolution is an obvious historical touchpoint for when the motor of the British economy really began to start turning. In the time between Thomas Newcomen inventing his atmospheric steam engine and the end of the nineteenth century, per capita incomes in England more than tripled. But previous prowess cannot sustain economic success into the twentieth century, let alone the twenty-first.

After the Second World War, the economy was characterised by reasonably strong and consistent economic growth, social democracy and corporatism. But this all came to a head with the malaise of the early 1970s, by the end of which the economic, and social, situation was desperate. Growth rates suffered and industrial unrest tore at the fabric of the nation.

The 1980s proved a turning point from this slump. Supply-side reforms, instigated by the Thatcher government, unshackled the British economy and gave the services sector in particular the jumpstart it sorely required. The Big Bang, ushered in by the Financial Services Act 1986, cemented London as the world's financial centre. Labour market and tax reforms made the UK a far more attractive proposition in which to do business, and net inflows of foreign direct investment into the country skyrocketed under her premiership. The spirit of this agenda was maintained by both the Major and Blair governments. Optimism coursed through the British economy in a way that seemed unimaginable just several years prior. From 1992 to 2007, there were sixteen years of unbroken economic growth, with output typically growing by around 2.5 per cent to three per cent per annum.

The point here is not to fetishise either the Industrial Revolution or the economic transformation of the 1980s. There has been a lot of talk in recent years about the idea of relaunching the Royal Yacht *Britannia* as a way of establishing Britain's international credentials, which is worthy and laudable. In its day, the Royal Yacht symbolised our shipbuilding prowess and our mercantile tradition. But in 2023, a yacht is not going to cut it. We cannot rely on nineteenth-century technology to sell the promise of twenty-first-century Britain.

Karaoke Thatcherism, beloved by some Conservative Party leadership hopefuls, is no panacea for our current travails either. Privatisation, deregulation and the shift to professional services, the formula of the 1980s, cannot be replicated. Rather, both successful episodes in our economic history point to the need to reinvent ourselves continually in order to stay competitive and to thrive. Today, the UK is one of the world's leading economies but is at risk of falling behind, precisely when our competitors have stepped up several gears to secure leadership positions in new industries.

Fifteen years after the global financial crisis, with the City of London less profitable than it once was, and North Sea oil output naturally declining, the UK needs a new economic model underpinned by a political philosophy that works, to drive innovation to counter the trend of poor productivity growth since 2009. Average UK real household income is broadly unchanged since 2007, just before the banking crisis, according to the Office for National Statistics. Household income per capita across OECD countries increased by twenty per cent between the first quarter of 2007, and the third quarter of 2022, but it only rose six per cent in the UK, according to the OECD. Low-income households in the UK are now 22 per cent poorer than their counterparts in France. Poor productivity, low growth and high inequality is not just bad for our prosperity as a nation, but it risks undermining the legitimacy of our wider economic system.

The state of the UK stock market makes the point further: all of the top ten UK firms by market capitalisation were founded before the year 2000. In the US, however, seven of their top ten were either built or scaled since then – including brands such as Tesla and Meta. Today, New York has usurped London as the centre of the financial world, while other locations – such as Singapore, Hong Kong and Dubai – are rapidly making inroads. The UK share of the global banking industry has shrunk enormously in the last two decades, with the number of top firms based in the UK declining too.

The Brexit referendum has also thrown the longstanding problems of the British economy into sharp relief. As Jonathan Haskel, an external member of the Bank of England's Monetary Policy Committee points out, a wave of investment 'stopped in its tracks' in 2016 following the vote, which explains why the UK suffered more of a productivity slowdown than other large economies. The implication of this is clear: the next wave of economic growth cannot replicate the winning policy prescription of the past, but requires the intellectual approach associated with the centre right of British politics to take a long and serious look at the structure of our economy, and our response to a world in which technology and innovation are an integral part of statecraft. Identifying new sources of growth, a vision of how to succeed and securing sovereignty in key industries is a non-negotiable path for the UK, because the next wave of growth cannot replicate the winning formula of the past, and success for the next generation and a continued global position of the country rests on the policy approach of today.

Vision for the future

Britain has significant competitive advantages, from an entrepreneurial can-do spirit, to excellent universities, and a strong scientific foundation, and the secret to a prosperous future lies in turning these assets into the engine of the British economy.

But the mindset of the populist left, for whom new technologies are a threat to workers rather than engines of economic and social progress, will not succeed. In a self-described radical speech responding to a report on the rise of robotics and artificial intelligence, Jeremy Corbyn's proposed solution was for workers to control the robots, to prevent a powerful and wealthy few benefiting from them.

Nor can the contradictory positions of the populist right, talking up 'Global Britain', while resisting collaboration with geographically proximate allies; seeing scientific endeavour through the peculiar lens of English nationalism, rather than a long painstaking process in which success comes from international collaboration; prioritising boosterism and celebrating the past, without the knowledge that the success of the past rests on bold and long-term decisions taken decades ago, and our future success rests on making important decisions now. And while political symbolism matters, it is no substitute for hard-headed policymaking based on an honest assessment of our strengths and weaknesses as a country.

Creating a dedicated science and innovation department with a Secretary of State is a welcome intervention. The department needs the vision and budget to make a success of its role in Whitehall. One way to conceive of the model for our economy as a whole is: much like it became the platform for finance and professional services, becoming a platform for science and innovation in the twenty-first century will deliver great rewards.

As a model for the entire British economy, openness to international collaboration with EU members and non-EU members, and creating new structures to deepen collaboration around the world, is vital. Secondly, a financial ecosystem that funds and commercialises the best research, and backs the growth of private and listed companies. Thirdly, an institutional and regulatory architecture that supports sensible risk-taking. Fourthly, an openness to the brightest and the best, the talented and the entrepreneurial, making Britain their home and the place to turn dreams into reality. Fifthly, no sensible discussion on economic growth can fail to take into account the planning system, because to a great extent, 'architecture is destiny'.

A glimpse into one aspect of the future of the UK as a platform for collaboration was provided by Dame Kate Bingham, when she, rightly, praised the announcement of the government's partnering with BioNtech to trial innovative vaccines in the UK. Trialling the game-changing approach of mRNA vaccines, which promise to protect patients against cancer in the same way as mRNA vaccines protect against Covid-19, put Britain at the forefront of a medical moonshot. Collaboration between the private and the public sector, and leveraging the NHS database is an example of the platform in action. As Dame Kate puts it 'if the trial is successful, it could change the whole landscape of how cancer is diagnosed and treated, enhancing the quality of millions of lives, and potentially saving the NHS billions'.

We also need to make the most of our openness to ideas. We should learn from the sharp-eyed heroes of the Industrial Revolution and think not just how we commercialise our own technology, but what we can learn and borrow from the best research around the world.

Galvanising private capital

In the scramble for dominance of emerging technologies, big budgets to support moonshots, strengthening innovation ecosystems and galvanising private-sector capital to build globally competitive businesses will be essential. Yet, the UK has a very middling record on investment in science, as defined by spending on R&D as a percentage of GDP when compared to other developing nations. Recently updated figures show that the UK

spends around 2.4 per cent of GDP on R&D, roughly similar to
that of France – and the European Union in general. But this is
still lower than the world average (2.63%) and the OECD average (2.93%), and ranks a long way behind R&D powerhouses
such as Germany (3.14%), Japan (3.26), the United States
(3.45%) and the Republic of Korea (4.81%).[1]

There is, however, reason for optimism. Successive
Chancellors have signalled their support over the last several years for the target of increasing the amount of money
spent on R&D. In 2022, the government announced a budget
for public R&D spending of close to £40 billion to be spent
between 2022 and 2025. New funding structures, not least
the Advanced Research and Invention Agency (ARIA), could
revolutionise particularly long-term and speculative research.
Without doubt, these developments will help in boosting the
quality and quantity of science and innovation carried out in
the UK.

At the other end of the funding barbell, while huge strides
have been made by successive governments, at the earliest
stages of funding for startups, a structural weakness in the
system is significantly less entrepreneurial capital available to
British entrepreneurs to build companies to scale and compete. In the tough space of autonomous driving, Oxbotica,
spun out of Oxford University, raised £140 million over five
investment rounds. Aurora, its US competitor, raised nearly
ten times more in the same time frame, and therefore had
better odds to succeed. Deepmind, which Alphabet acquired
before it reached unicorn status, is a case in point of great companies being sold before they have reached their full potential.

Outside a sale, technology, life sciences and climate tech
companies, which need to raise significant capital to grow,
rely on foreign investors. In any funding round north of £100
million, it is exceptionally rare for a British institution to lead
the round. US, Canadian, Australian, Sovereign Wealth Funds
all lead rounds, but never British or European institutions,

with significant implications for the political decisions on the board, particularly governance and where the headquarters of the company is eventually located. An important lesson from the turbulence of the last few years is that technical sovereignty matters: from vaccine production, to payment systems and internet connectivity, having governance and control over strategic sectors matters.

To date, the Oxford–AstraZeneca vaccine has not been approved in the United States. Without the good efforts of Elon Musk and the United States government, Europe would be unable to supply Ukraine with internet connectivity, which Starlink provides. At the onset of the war, Oneweb, the British-backed satellite start-up, needed the Russian Soyuz for launch purposes. The unprecedented weaponisation of Visa and Mastercard payment rails – without a public debate on materiality – as part of the sanctions package against Russia, again makes the point.

For economic and security reasons, a long hard look at the not too unfamiliar cycle where the taxpayer funds research, which is then commercialised, with taxpayer incentives, and foreign investors exploit the growth and commercial opportunity when the company has been de-risked.

As a comparison, the Yale Endowment Fund allocates roughly 23 per cent of the endowment to venture capital, to back the growth companies of the future. In Europe, pension funds allocate less than 0.02 per cent to back the future growth. The UK Financing Gap report by Lakestar, a pan-European Venture Capital firm and McKinsey, the strategy consulting firm, notes that for UK growth to move from the current range of 0.5–1.0 per cent to 2–3 per cent, more than £75 billion growth financing per year until 2040 is needed to finance the growth companies of the future.

Institutional and regulatory architecture

Availability of finance while necessary is not the only driver of entrepreneurial decisions on where to locate. Strong and stable pro-innovation institutions enable capital to flow in the right direction. Our universities are an intrinsic part of the innovation economy, and constraining public funding as part of the 'culture wars' or to punish universities for being pro-Remain institutions is short-sighted and will damage the country in the long term.

Our best universities are not just powerhouses of research – they are also deeply connected to their local and national businesses, and to their community. There is an important geographical angle to consider. It is no surprise that many of the UK's most successful publicly funded labs and institutions are in the Oxford–Cambridge–London triangle, because we rightly fund research on the basis of excellence and not political patronage, and one corollary of that is that the most successful universities have consistently punched above their weight in winning further research funding. But it is important that we recognise that, when it comes to innovation, there is life outside the Golden Triangle.

Indeed, sometimes the private sector seems quicker to realise it than public research funders. As the innovation expert Tom Forth has pointed out, there are parts of the West Midlands and the North West where business invests heavily in R&D but the public sector seems not to. Turning our universities into powerhouses of economic growth in their area, and to ensure we back innovation wherever it may be is how we build real strength in places across the country. But universities are not the only institutions that can drive innovation. We should also consider how our regulatory systems can encourage innovation, by making sure that our rules keep up with the pace of technology and business change.

Businesses will set up and thrive where regulations provide

more of a tailwind than a headwind. From the ethics of artificial intelligence, to drones and air traffic systems; from regulating cryptocurrencies to data used for innovation in healthcare; from the Contracts for Difference framework that unlocked off-shore wind energy, to artificial proteins, and the framework for regulating gig economy workers: in almost every emerging technology sector regulation will play a vital role in determining whether innovative businesses can succeed. Here too the race is on between countries, with nations such as Singapore playing an active enabling role for artificial proteins and cryptocurrencies. For the UK platform to succeed, designing the rules of the game for business and the economy that support the spirit of adventure is a table stake. Regulators should pay greater regard to being innovation-maximisers, as opposed to just pure risk-minimisers. They should consider how to enable new entrepreneurs, instead of simply overseeing existing incumbents. There should be more opportunities to challenge outdated legislation which holds back emergent sectors. A spirit of 'permissionless innovation' should replace the precautionary principle.

The economist and regulation expert John Fingleton has previously proposed that the UK creates a so-called 'N+1 regulator', which could give licences to disruptive entrants across the entire economy. In a recent speech he outlined how regulating on a cross-sector basis, rather than sector-by-sector basis could enable us to reduce regulatory capture by incumbents, be able to learn from different sectors, streamline regulatory approval processes, and also be able to better stand up to political questions about how to balance risk and reward.

For a contingent of British politicians and commentators, the proverbial bonfire of red tape is all we need to transform the UK into a modern and innovative economy. There may be a grain of truth in this, but it obscures a more sophisticated analysis of the problem at hand. What we really require is a smarter view of how to regulate; what frameworks, what mechanisms, what institutions are going to position Britain as a leader in the eyes of the industries that will shape the coming decades.

The UK should aspire to be a global testbed, where ingenious companies and entrepreneurs are welcomed and encouraged to launch and trial whatever innovation it is they have developed. Not everything will succeed, but it is only by providing these fertile conditions that we can hope to find out which might. And, in doing so, Britain would become the first place to benefit from and capture the economic and societal advantages of such innovation.

The brightest and the best

Brexit cast a shadow over Britain's otherwise tolerant attitude to immigration. For some the vote was a vote to close ourselves off from the world. But we should be proud that so many of the best and brightest from other countries choose to bring their knowledge and skills to Britain, and we should recognise that our economy is stronger for it.

As a platform, Britain should be the place where the sharpest minds can come to work on the biggest challenges. If you are, in the words of the musical *Hamilton*, 'young, scrappy and hungry', with the desire and talent to change the world, you should find a welcome here. Because countries with the insurgent mindset are the ones that succeed. Hard data bears this out, however, with analysts at Beauhurst finding that 40 per cent of Britain's unicorn firms have an immigrant founder, while the think tank The Entrepreneurs Network has found that half of Britain's 100 fastest growing companies have a foreign-born founder or co-founder. While these figures relate to companies in all sectors – not just ones focused on science and technology – many nevertheless fall into that category.

Put simply, people matter. If the United Kingdom is to be the advanced and powerful economy it should be aspiring to be, we need to make sure we have the best possible people right here, right now.

To its credit, the government has recently made some welcome steps here. The High Potential Individual Visa (HPIV) allows graduates from prestigious universities to move to the UK for up to two years without a job offer. But even this visa is not without fault. Its methodology does not necessarily capture all of the sorts of institutions that we would want it to – in particular, it has been found to exclude several Indian Institutes of Technology and other STEM-focused universities. In the United States, sixty of the CEOs of the Fortune 500 are of Indian heritage, studied in hyper-competitive India Institutions and elite US universities, including Satya Nadella, Chairman and CEO of Microsoft, and Sunder Pichai, CEO of Alphabet and Google.

Immigrants have started more than half (319 of 582) of America's start-up companies valued at $1billion or more (unicorns), according to analysis by the National Foundation for American Policy. Nearly two-thirds of the US billion-dollar companies were founded or co-founded by immigrants or the children of immigrants.

Britain is already endowed with its fair share of brilliant minds, but that is not to say we would not benefit from having more. For the migrating innovators themselves, Britain might also be the ticket they need to truly fulfil their potential, whether that's on a university campus, inside a laboratory, or working for – or founding – one of our growing number of technology driven companies. We should be unapologetic in giving the brightest, the best, the talented and the entrepreneurial the opportunity to rise in Britain.

Planning

One broad umbrella of regulations that are so deleterious to innovation and economic growth is planning. By this I mean the rules that effectively determine what can be built and where. The UK has some of the tightest planning laws in the world. These rules limit the supply of new construction – whether that's homes we live in, commercial premises to do business from, lab space to conduct research in, or the energy, transport and digital infrastructure that underpin a successful economy. And, as any economist worth their salt will tell you, when supply of a good is fixed but demand for it keeps rising, the cost only goes in one direction – upwards.

How obviously this impacts science and innovation varies. At the more straightforward end of the spectrum, if lab space is expensive, that also drives up the cost of doing research – and rents for lab space in places like Oxford, Cambridge and London are generally highly elevated relative to American or European equivalent locations. At its worst, scientists find there literally isn't the space to carry out scientific experiments. Research either gets carried out at greater expense – or not at all (or, more likely, in another country instead).

A less obvious way in which our planning rules stifle science is by limiting the supply of homes. Even if we had ample lab space, it would mean little if scientists couldn't afford to live suitably nearby. Again, rents and house prices in and around the areas where Britain's scientific strengths lie are significantly inflated – pricing out would-be innovators.

By making it difficult to build transport infrastructure, planning laws hinder the ability for innovative individuals to physically move around to collaborate and exchange ideas. By making it difficult to build digital infrastructure, planning laws hinder the ability for them to do so online – something of pronounced importance in the post-pandemic world. By making it difficult to build energy infrastructure, we ramp up the costs of literally powering innovation, while also closing down opportunities for scientists to contribute towards the Green energy revolution.

Conclusion

Today's industrial landscape is fundamentally altered. Since 2000, the UK has given away leadership positions in key sectors such as financial services, energy and telecommunications, fuelled by the financial crisis and further impacted by Brexit. New industries in life sciences, sustainable energy, and technology are gaining in importance, and advanced nations are orienting their economies to lead, because of the huge implications for economic prosperity and security.

If Britain is to make its way in this new world, we need a strategic state, under-pinned by a clear set of values based on openness, pragmatism and a hard-headed approach to our national self-interest. Populism of the left or the right will lead the country to an economic dead-end. Muddling through is not a credible option. Openness to international collaboration with the EU and beyond, pro-innovation institutions including regulation of emerging technologies, a positive approach to immigration, and grasping the thorny nettle of planning reform might not stir populist hearts but are essential ingredients for success.

Other nations have set out their stall with 'new industrial strategies'. The UK cannot compete on every field and shouldn't aim to; but a true platform for innovation will help establish the UK's place in the world, and our future prosperity.

8

The Future of Climate and Energy Policy
Amber Rudd

The clue is in the name. Conservatives. What do we seek to do? It's as if the Conservative Party political name was invented to lead the campaign to protect the planet against dangerous climate change. Margaret Thatcher was the first world leader to call for international action in 1990, when she said: 'The danger of global warming is as yet unseen, but real enough for us to make changes and sacrifices, so that we do not live at the expense of future generations.' This is still an accurate summary of the challenge, and the consequences of inaction.

Akin to the industrialisation of the nineteenth century, the move from fossil fuels to renewables has gone from an urgent need to protect the planet from over-heating, to a global arms race to provide the technologies and solutions of the future for clean power. We know that this clean power is coming. The question is how soon, and which countries are going to be the leaders and therefore the winners on the new sources of the future. Combining bold leadership, conservation and ambitious economic development should be at the heart of a liberal Conservative manifesto.

A strong start under Cameron

In 2008 Gordon Brown's Labour government put forward the Climate Change Act. They initially proposed calling for the UK to reduce emissions from 1990 levels by 50 per cent by 2050. But it wasn't just to be a 'commitment', the Bill carried implementation and transparency requirements. It required successive governments to show progress through reporting on 'carbon budgets' every five years and it set up the independent Committee on Climate Change to oversee progress.

We are now on the 6th Carbon Budget and the Committee on Climate Change is vocal and critical of current progress. It has legal standing. It has teeth. It is delivering as it was intended as the 'truth teller' to government. In some countries the party of the right was and remains less ambitious than the left to acknowledge and address climate change. In some of these countries the party of the right is positively hostile to measures against climate change.

The US Republicans are staunch opposers of recent renewable energy policy changes in the US, not just because of partisan differences but because of their support for some of the dirtiest of fossil fuels. Who can forget Sarah Palin, one-time vice-presidential candidate, with her 'drill baby drill' slogan, and Donald Trump's early move after election in 2016 to withdraw from the Paris Climate Agreement? And, in Europe, the most populist leaders on the right are also the ones most unwilling to engage with the climate change agenda.

In the UK, however, the Conservative Party in 2008 didn't just support Labour's Climate Change Act but pushed the governing party to go further. The initial 50 per cent ambition (reduction of carbon emissions from a 1990 level) was upped to 80 per cent under goading from David Cameron. His Conservative leadership was central to establishing the Conservatives as both conservative on the environment and ambitious in the energy and climate change agenda. His leadership in 2006 kicked off with a visit to the Arctic to showcase the danger of the melting ice cap and to capture his commitment to the climate change agenda. And, in the general election of 2010, he urged the voters to 'think green, vote blue', allowing this writer and nervous first-time parliamentary candidate in Hastings to add 'ditch Brown, and choose Amber'. The public always call for political parties to work together to address major long-term issues. The Climate Change Act and its ambition was evidence of that happening.

Watering down the Green agenda

The coalition of 2010 to 2015 was a Liberal Conservative government. Not surprisingly the Secretary of State for Energy and Climate Change was from the Liberal Democrat side of the coalition. During those years former Lib Dem leadership candidate Chris Huhne MP was succeeded by current Lib Dem leader Ed Davey MP. Those governing years revealed the difficulties of delivering, rather than just campaigning, on an ambitious agenda.

Although the majority of Conservative MPs during that period supported the plans, there was a cabal who did not. This group overlapped with 'Brexit' supporters and would become the MPs who were most dedicated to leaving the EU. The Venn diagram of opposing climate change action and supporting leaving the EU is pretty conclusive – the most stringent climate change deniers are the lead Brexiters. It was John Hayes, a leading Brexiter, who as a junior minister for energy in the coalition announced he was going to put the 'coal' back into coalition.

It is a mind set on the right of conservatism that rubbishes expertise, that is suspicious of change, and is nostalgic for an imaginary perfect past. In both climate change and in our relationship with the EU, the hard right of the Conservative Party stood against David Cameron's liberal centrist approach.

Although David Cameron's leadership in the coalition and, briefly, as head of a majority Conservative government did achieve some groundbreaking wins for cleaner energy, the balance sheet is not entirely in his favour. On the one hand, the UK did seize world leadership in delivering off-shore wind and, during my time as Secretary of State for Energy and Climate Change, became the first Western country to put a date on ending unabated coal. On the other hand, the pressures of the electorate led to reductions of some climate change policies that slowed down some of the positive changes being made.

When rising energy bills became the major domestic priority, David Cameron called for part of the 'Green' charge on people's bills to be reduced. Those funds had been allocated to pay for insulating people's homes. It was a costly mistake for many households who didn't get the energy saving support that would have reduced their bills, and lowered the UK's carbon emissions. But Cameron clearly assessed that he needed to make that change to keep the voters with him. Their bills were getting too large and were impacting on their views on this government. A politician has to maintain public support. It is a reminder that politicians may know what to do, but they may struggle to get elected after they have done it.

The case for climate action has only accelerated during the past ten years. Not only is the science clearer than ever, but the visible manifestation of the dangers are around us all the time. The floods in India and California and the fires in Australia have been regularly terrifying the world as they are shown on our TVs. Voters have become more supportive. A liberal Conservative policy can be bolder. We can now have on-shore wind (effectively banned under David Cameron due to electoral pressure) because of a recent shift from public scepticism to public backing for a broader roll-out of wind turbines across the UK countryside.

Of course, every politician has to choose their own priorities. But addressing the long-term challenge of clean energy and the opportunities that go with it, should be at the top of a politician's agenda. Stable government is the prerequisite to deliver the long-term energy infrastructure change. Investors require a stable regime to have confidence that policy and tax rates can be relied on. That's been somewhat missing in the UK since 2015. Too many PMs, too many elections and frankly too much uncertainty – made even worse by the consequences of Russia's invasion of Ukraine. The huge rise in energy prices led to 'windfall' taxes, which further damaged confidence in the UK as an investment location. One board member of a leading global investor drily told me that they consider the UK to have the same political risk as Nigeria.

The only way to mitigate against this, or at least to reduce the perceived risk, is to demonstrate that political leaders and their party members share the ambition. Our four Conservative PMs in the past seven years have had different degrees of enthusiasm for addressing a clean energy future. But none have slowed down the progress or explicitly taken the path of other Western right-wing parties by rubbishing the urgent need for action. None tried to withdraw from the Paris agreement for instance, as Trump had done. As a PM, Boris Johnson was a champion of clean energy and the environment (though he certainly had not been as a back bencher or even as Foreign Secretary). But under Boris Johnson the UK hosted the UN COP (Conference of the Parties) in Glasgow in 2022 and sought to push the ambition of the international community on addressing climate change.

But Johnson couldn't deliver the stability required to achieve real progress. Instead, he made endless promises about what would be done in a way that undermined confidence. If the target looks impossible it makes the whole strategy look absurd. For instance, he announced that the UK would build one nuclear power station a year. Considering the UK has just one under construction and one hovering around the starter gun and no further advanced project in the pipeline nobody believed him. Quite rightly. An essential ingredient of good policy is always going to be a partnership with the private sector to raise the vast amounts of capital needed. Good leadership, and stable government will bring that in. Announcements characterised by NIMTO (not in my term of office) will not achieve that.

Building on Paris

The Paris Agreement of 2015 was a success, despite the many conflicting interests around the world. The UK's role was not only to sign up to the ambitious plan, but to shape the world agreement and lobby, cajole and influence to make sure that our interests were well served from the final accord. The UK's diplomatic service was harnessed in support and the foreign service was on hand during the 2015 negotiations to assist. But the challenge of climate change is global. Our climate and energy policy should extend beyond our shores to the values and influence we can leverage to promote a global solution. We were able to do that in Paris in 2015 as we participated in, and in many instances, led the European response with lead UK negotiator, the great Pete Betts, at the helm.

Our role in the EU acted as a multiplier for our influence in achieving the final deal. It was the UK that led the partnership with the Small Island Nations, brilliantly co-chaired by Tony de Brum of the Marshall Islands. In the last few days of the Paris negotiations we added a more stretching target for limiting the increase in temperature not merely to a maximum of two per cent but rather to a much more challenging 1.5 per cent. Both those numbers are on the front of the final document. But seven years on it is the 1.5 per cent that is referred to. Regrettably, we no longer have that influence.

Influence and outcomes in international agreement are about working in blocs. Unless you are one of the great powers,

most significantly America, you are just one country trying
to be heard among many others. Although we can no longer
lead the EU, we can still use our diplomatic power, through
our embassies and high commissions, to try to shape other
countries' responses. A centrist Conservative government
must have the confidence to lean into Europe. We should find
a different way to influence. Despite being outside the EU we
must find a closer working relationship that allows us to share
ideas and work together in climate change. The hard right of
the Conservative Party is unlikely to ever support the soften-
ing of a relationship with Europe. It will only come from the
centre.

The challenge ahead

Fortunately, there are plenty of innovators focused on finding solutions for our need for abundant clean energy. From
direct air capture (literally sucking carbon out of the air) to
nuclear fusion, the UK has continued to invest in and provide
government-led support for new sources of clean energy.

We have shown that we can create an environment with tax,
subsidy and legislation that allows new investment and early
stage trials to flourish. The auctions for off-shore wind remain
a success at finding the right price for government not directly
to subsidise, but to guarantee a price that the electricity will be
bought at. This is what allows long-term international investors to participate and has allowed the sector to flourish. This,
together with bad weather and geography, is what has made us
European leaders in off-shore wind.

But recent legislation in the US, to be followed by a form
of 'copy cat' EU equivalent, will tempt manufacturers and
innovators away from the UK. The US Congressional Budget
Office estimates that the tax breaks offered from their Inflation
Reduction Act could pay out more than $350bn over ten years.

The so called 'IRA' is a huge bung towards more renewable energy and set up as an alternative to China's success in this sector. It is expressly intended to promote American sourcing and manufacturing. It is wide ranging, for instance covering transport and local small and medium companies, as well as individual household support for solar energy. For good measure, the US also passed the Chips Act in August 2022, which sets out to offer subsidies and support for the US semi-conductor industry.

The EU 'IRA' equivalent (which is still under discussion) will also be protectionist, in order not to lose out to the US. Already a major French solar manufacturer has cancelled plans to build a manufacturing centre in northern France and announced it will go to the US instead.

What should the UK response to these protectionist blocks be from a right of centre government? It must have an offer. It cannot be an outlier here. We cannot compete with the billions on offer from the US or the EU. Both these initiatives are designed to compete with China. We are not the target. We should seek to ally ourselves with one or both. We should come forward with our own offer – on skills and training. Providing the funding is only part of the challenge. The energy transition will devour experts needed for the clean brave new world. We still have some of the top universities. We should focus on being the training centre for the skills that the Americans and the EU are buying.

It will be complicated, what with tensions over work visas, and politicians wanting national subsidies to support local employment, but there is undoubtedly an opportunity here and it is worth the UK pursuing it. At a time when trust in poli-ticians is at record lows, I would make the case for ambition and urgency that is also realistic. I would hope that a liberal Conservative government could have the confidence and the knowledge to be frank about the challenges. That includes facing up to the role that oil and gas is currently playing. Only by being honest about the continued need for oil and gas, it is a *transition* after all, can we also reasonably call for a strategy that is ambitious for high standards and low emissions while extraction continues.

Any government facing up to the need for continued oil and gas has got to look at how to reduce carbon emissions despite that. The answer is to put more emphasis into carbon capture and storage. Climate change is not going to wait for us to stop using oil and gas, so we must invest in capturing the carbon at source.

Uniting the party behind net zero

Part of the challenge for the Conservatives to show leadership in this area is to take the whole party with it. Splits in the party are a defining characteristic of Conservative MPs. But maybe different factions of the party can be persuaded to support the same energy transition for different reasons? That was the motivation behind Liz Truss, our 49-day PM, commissioning Chris Skidmore MP to do a net zero review. To those of us committed to the need and the opportunities of net zero, it felt baffling that a review to prove the self-evident economic case was being requested by the new government.

But, since the report came out in January 2023, it has effectively contributed to the economic case behind the transition. The report demonstrates that the case for clean and renewable energy is not just good for the planet but good for the UK's economy. The 'antis' always object on cost, citing the need for cheaper dirty energy to support family budgets. The net zero review, however, blows that apart, revealing the inherent economic advantage for families, for industry and for leadership for the country. It calls for a speedier approach to delivering net zero, in industry and in homes. These would be supported by all wings of the Conservative Party. The disagreement in the end is likely to be about the speed of the transition.

And for a government report, it was unusual when it even received a warm welcome from the opposition. Just as Labour's Climate Change Act was welcomed and improved on by the Conservative opposition in 2008, the Skidmore review was welcomed, while calling for more ambition from the Labour opposition in 2023. An ambitious Conservative approach to net zero is going to be difficult for Labour to oppose. Even the Lib Dems struggled to oppose it. Their main criticism can be summed up as, 'yes, this, but faster . . .'

The difference, though, between a Conservative and Labour policy is one of where the cost lies. A net zero world will eventually have cheaper energy than currently (the sun and the wind have no overheads for us), although there are costs to get there. If we don't count the cost of carbon, then coal is cheap. The replacement sources are inevitably going to raise prices in the short term. The cost of reliable, clean, nuclear energy used to be considered high. Not any more compared to some of the reliable alternatives.

Under Labour who will pay this bill? With their plan for 'GB Energy' they seem to be tinkering with nationalisation, at least in part. Instead of creating the environment for business and investment they appear to be putting more of the costs on the tax payer. It's difficult to be sure because Keir Starmer is saying so little about what goes into 'GB Energy', but their emphasis is certainly not about stability and investment. It's much more about attacking big businesses and high-earning energy companies. A good example of the dangers of putting costs of major energy infrastructure onto the taxpayer would have been Hinkley Point. The original estimate for the construction cost was £18bn. It is now £32bn. That is not a taxpayer cost, at least not in the UK, as the owners EDF are largely owned by the French government.

The trilemma

We need energy that is not just low in emissions and cost, but is also reliable and secure. What is called the trilemma – think of it like a Rubik's Cube: if you try to get one side right then the other sides get muddled up. We have to balance all three needs: carbon reduction, cost and security.

Bill Gates's book on climate is optimistic about the way human ingenuity can find the solutions. And he is also honest about the short-term costs, the so called 'green premium'. Even now, if you want to secure your personal electricity supply through solar PV there will be a capital outlay that is not for the faint hearted (hence the huge American largesse). And more if you choose to have a home battery for storage.

Who pays for the 'green premium'? The tax payer, the bill payer or the manufacturer responding to new legislation?

Energy prices were already soaring in the West before Russia invaded the Ukraine. But the war has revealed the West's lazy and dangerous reliance on Russian oil and gas. We have been scrabbling to adjust and the prices have reflected the sudden withdrawal of Russian supply. It's put the emphasis on security of supply and made everyone an expert in the challenges of the transition. That must be a good thing. If the public are better informed and feel more invested in the choices politicians make then we are likely to get more realistic leadership. As with so many policies, there are trade offs in the decisions being made. Airing those will help with lasting support.

Conclusion

A Conservative climate change and energy policy can only be successful and distinctive from Labour if it can recover the trust of business and investors. David Cameron's Conservatives explicitly focused on securing business and investor confidence.

Reducing corporation taxes from 2010 to 2016 was deliberate to attract international investors. Even the pro Chinese policy of George Osborne was partially to secure their investment in Hinkley Point.

Although Boris Johnson was committed to the agenda, without the support of business he could not advance the plans. The 'F***' business comment lived on among investors for longer than he or his government admitted. The 'nostalgia' Brexit supporting group of Conservative MPs are hardly interested in either climate change or the opportunities it offers. And, just as they will not accept the evidence of damage being done by Brexit to the UK, and particularly to our SMEs, they will not change their views on climate change and energy.

A party that delivers, by leaving the EU, a body blow to British industry and trade, will struggle to be able to harness the value of business and direct investment to support the vast amounts of money for the energy transition. Even now, businesses find it exasperating that the current Conservative government and its MPs continue to rubbish their actual experiences of the difficulties of trade, having left the EU. There is no acknowledgement of that change. Trust, once lost, cannot be quickly regained.

To succeed, a liberal Conservative policy has got to have straightforward and reassuring conversations with business to harness their support and capital. It must offer stability and honesty. It must acknowledge the Brexit challenges and seek ways of supporting business that are based on listening to them, not political ideology. It has to win the trust of the international investors, the entrepreneurs, the business leaders that are going to make the transition a reality. That should not be too much to ask of a truly Conservative Party.

9

A pro-European and
pro-Devolution Agenda
Michael Heseltine

With the following words *The Daily Mail* celebrated our departure from the European Union:

> This is a magnificent day for Great Britain. We should celebrate our new freedom – and pay tribute to the countless ordinary Britons who showed so much more wisdom than the self-serving political and financial elites that for too long have ignored their anxieties and aspirations.

I was a fan of the late David English, a great editor of that newspaper from 1979 to 1992, who could be forgiven if he felt the pro Europe paper he edited was unfairly reflected in those words.

The *Daily Mail* headline at the time of our exit proclaimed 'Now we can lead Europe.' This was exactly what so many of those so-called political and financial elites wanted to hear, even though it reflected a status that was not available. It was in much smaller type in an inside page that in March 2023 they reported the Office for Budget Responsibility conclusion that British output had reduced by about four per cent as a direct result of our leaving the EU.

By the early 1970s Britain had grown tired of its post-war economic struggle, its colonial battles to maintain an outdated imperial hegemony quite beyond its means. There was a growing awareness that the special relationship with the United States was a concept more real on this side of the Atlantic than the other. We joined a club whose rationale and motivation was to share sovereignty and replace that narrow-minded nationalism that had characterised European history and engaged France and Germany in three wars in three-quarters of a century.

The Europe we were joining was founded by people with an overriding determination that wars in Europe must never happen again. The first step was the plan by the French Foreign Minister Robert Schuman to create an international agreement to bring the war-making industries of coal, iron and steel under shared rules. This became the European Coal and Steel Community, created by the Treaty of Paris, and was the first supra-national agreement between Belgium, France, Italy, Luxembourg, The Netherlands and West Germany.

From there, Jean Monnet led the way to establish the European Economic Community, created by the Treaty of Rome in 1957 and signed by the same six nations. Winston Churchill had earlier reflected the mood in one of his most famous post-war speeches when he proclaimed that we must create a kind of United States of Europe. Note the use of the word 'we'. He did not say 'they'. At that time, we could have had a leadership role. Our defiance in standing alone from 1939 to 1941 and our contribution to the restoration of liberty in Europe gave us a unique opportunity. But it was not to be.

At the Messina Conference of 1955 Paul-Henri Spaak, the then Belgian Prime Minister, confronted us with the choice – join us or leave us. His words were provoked by the inability of the British officials to join in the negotiations. One of them explained this to Michael Charlton in his BBC radio programme *The Price of Victory*. 'We could get no instructions from London.' From that moment, Britain could talk of partnership, and an influential one at that, but never leadership. That concept was relevant only in the headlines of the national media of the individual countries.

We were not alone in our reluctance to share sovereignty. Six nations signed up to the Messina Conference in 1955. In 1960, seven other countries – Austria, Denmark, Norway, Portugal, Sweden, Switzerland, and the United Kingdom signed up to a looser free trade area – EFTA .Thus, Europe came to resemble a committed core and a sceptic fringe.

Half a century later, Europe looks entirely different. In 1992 the Maastricht Treaty had taken the integration of Europe a step closer and in 1994 the European Economic Area Agreement brought Iceland, Liechtenstein and Norway into the rules of a single market. The European Union consisted of 27 countries including four of the original EFTA group and Finland. The EU now has a queue of applicant nations.

The harms of Brexit

'We got our country back. Oven ready. The easiest trade deal in history. Bring back control.' Such were the Leavers' fantasies. Those of us who opposed Brexit asked the obvious but inconvenient question. What does this mean? How can they be achieved? Are they anything except empty and totally misleading phrases to deceive an electorate frustrated by years of frozen living standards?

Immediately after the referendum I wrote an article in the *Mail on Sunday* urging the Prime Minister to put the leading Brexiteers in charge of the proclaimed new opportunities that Britain would need to exploit to compensate for the obvious disadvantages of leaving the world's single biggest free-trade area. Speed and decisiveness might conceivably have delivered the promised new beginning. Although not apparent to me

– or, indeed, to almost half of the population – it was reasonable to assume that those who led the Brexit campaign knew what they actually wanted to do and how to do it. They did not.

Boris Johnson became Foreign Secretary, Liam Fox was given Trade, and David Davis responsibility for exiting the European Union. This proved less than the forecast triumph. Boris Johnson ejected the Prime Minister, consigned his two former colleagues to the back benches and promised his own oven-ready deal to 'get Brexit done'. This came as something of a surprise to those of us who thought that that was what he and his two colleagues were supposed to have been doing. Jacob Rees-Mogg was appointed to the Cabinet to lead the charge as Minister for Brexit Opportunities, while Liz Truss travelled the world, signing the trade deals in growth markets, within which we were told we could pick off the low-hanging fruit at our leisure.

Now seven years since the referendum and well over three years after the country voted substantially 'to get Brexit done', times throughout the world have been unrelentingly hard. Covid, Putin and the resultant economic crisis were largely responsible but only Britain added Brexit to the toxic mix. A wide range of forecasts show how much harm Brexit is doing. Inevitably these are dismissed by those who habitually discount whatever evidence or expertise fails to suit their story. Such was the fate of warnings from the IMF, the World Bank, the OECD, the Bank of England, the Office for Budget Responsibility, the Institute for Fiscal Studies and the Treasury. Indeed, Liz Truss was so sure that the OBR would raise the alarm about the effect her proposed budget would have on the markets that she refused to consult them.

But markets have a habit of revealing the truth. Take, for example, the currency markets. In 2016, before the referendum, the pound was trading at 1.48 to the dollar and 1.30 to the Euro. The pound fell to 1.36 between the time the polling stations closed and markets reopened the next morning. It has drifted much lower since then. The euro dropped seven per cent over the same time and is lower still at the time of writing. This was grist to the inflationary mill and great news for foreigners anxious to buy up British companies.

As the evidence accumulates with the passage of time and as more and more people take to the media to explain their experience of increased cost, paperwork and delay, the public mood has changed. The latest polls show that a significant majority now believes Brexit was a mistake. In October 2022 an IPSOS MORI poll reported that most people believed that Brexit had damaged the economy, while less than a quarter thought the opposite.

As we approach the next election, both leading parties are hypnotised by the hard core of Brexit voters, mainly in the north of England, who delivered the government its majority. The Brexit press and the fear that Nigel Farage will return to lead the Reform party with his populist rhetoric led the mainstream parties to embrace the delusion that Brexit can be made to work. Brexit is a consequence of the populist shift to the nationalist right personified by Trump in America, Le Pen in France and Farage here. There is a common cause and it is the frustration widely felt by those whose living standards have failed to match their expectations and past experience.

Not so splendid isolation

The centre right agenda today must be to persuade electors that solutions depend on cooperation not confrontation, on healing the wounds in society not picking away at them with all the inflammatory language the headline writers love.

It is often argued that a significant contributor to anti-Europeanism is that the original case for Brexit was founded almost entirely on economics. This argument is exemplified by the transformation of the European Economic Community into the European Union by the Maastricht Treaty. The economic argument was and remains an important part of the case but it was never the whole case or, initially, the driving force. It was the desire to live in peace that galvanised the European movement.

German industrial self-interest in pursuit of wider markets explains the subsidies she was prepared to pay. France was determined to preserve her rural structure and thus prevent a significant migration to the towns and cities. It may well have suited those arguing for our accession to the European Community in 1973 to emphasise the economic arguments that could help us escape from the reputation as Europe's laggard, but the purpose and direction of a united Europe was always there and so remains. It aligns with British self-interest. Our foreign, defence, environment, cultural and academic interests are interwoven with our economic performance. The damage caused by severing our industrial and commercial links with our neighbours and largest market undermines our standing and influence with them and with the wider world.

I do not intend to speculate about our diplomatic response to crises yet to come. I find it difficult to imagine a decisive British voice if the rest of Europe disagrees. Our voice will always be louder where, as a result of sharing sovereignty, our influence is felt through a like-minded power block, whether it be the UN, NATO or the EU. In the real world there is nothing splendid about isolation. For most of my life I have lived under the umbrella of the NATO alliance. As Defence Secretary I argued for and believed that the combination of an independent deterrent and commitment to a US-led NATO provide the West with the best possible defence against aggression. Pax Americana has lasted now for approaching eighty years, surviving the sadly short era when Russia appeared to be less of a threat. The invasion of Ukraine has demonstrated the wisdom of that policy and led to a significant increase in the size of the Alliance, a consequence diametrically the opposite of what Putin intended.

Yet, however much one is grateful for the NATO alliance, one cannot assume that there will always be a coincidence between British, European and American self-interest. America acted decisively to end the Anglo-French invasion of Egypt in 1956. President Reagan was torn between the interests of his country in South America and those of this country in the Falklands. It was Secretary of Defence Cap Weinberger who tilted the argument in our favour. I was in the room when President Reagan assured Mrs Thatcher that he had no intention of putting his troops into Grenada, a British colony just twenty-four hours before he did so. Years after I ceased to be Defence Secretary I was in the United States on St Patrick's Day and watched the scale of the annual celebration. This was not just support for one of that country's many immigrant groups. The presence of the American Marines demonstrated an altogether greater significance. There should have been little surprise in a post-Brexit world that American reaction would focus on the Irish question.

No one can predict the changing nature of American politics. Those charged with anticipating the contingencies that will create tomorrow must ask. Will America always come? They came and played a decisive role in the First World War but not until 1917. Memories of that horrendous war influenced American opinion decisively and understandably. In the American presidential elections of 1940 President Roosevelt was forced by his Republican opponents to give and then reinforce a categorical assurance that he would not commit troops to another European war. He never reneged on that promise. In 1941 the Japanese attacked Pearl Harbour and very shortly after, Hitler declared war on the United States.

President Macron is right to argue that Europe should do more to think through the basis of European defence if some future United States administration reduces or reprioritises its overseas commitments. Indeed, the more serious we on this side of the Atlantic take our defence interests the more likely it is that America will continue to support the present arrangements. If the NATO alliance holds, America will lead it. Over the long term, one cannot avoid the difficult question of what command structure would replace them. Would twenty-seven national military structures be expected to defend their individual territory?

A responsible approach to immigration

If defence is at the heart of foreign policy, the most intractable aspect of foreign policy today is immigration. Certainly, no issue is more central to an understanding of the state of the world in general and Brexit in particular. Living standards in this country froze and then fell after the financial collapse of 2008. People wanted change and the Brexiteers ruthlessly exploited the most explosive issues – foreigners, Brussels, forms, immigrants, anyone, anything that shifted the blame onto those who could not answer back in a rerun of history's most toxic exploitation of tribe, race and nationalism.

Nowhere is the consequence of modern communications systems more evident than in the surge of immigration with its destabilising consequences across the world. Conditions are being created that justify their citizens' appeals for asylum. We have been generous in our response to people from Hong Kong, Afghanistan and Ukraine. There are wars in Yemen, Syria and Sudan as brutal as any in history.

But, in addition, there is the mobile phone. In any part of the world, in real time, the young and energetic can see how we live. There may be deeply held feelings about poverty and hunger in our domestic political debate here but anyone with such a phone in the third world can observe our living standards and see them as those about which they can only dream.

It is going to get worse. Climate change and rising sea levels threaten millions of people living in coastal communities with the need to relocate. Flooding adds to the problem. Large numbers of those affected are in Commonwealth countries. As the crisis develops there will be growing reference to what the Commonwealth means and the sacrifices its members have made on our behalf. The fifty thousand people who this year risked their lives to cross the channel are a microcosm of the problem. The resentment of this infringement of our sovereign right to control our borders is focused on the French. These immigrants are not French. They are a small part of the masses from Syria, Iran, Iraq and many other poor countries who crossed French frontiers from the south and east.

This is a European problem and I believe it needs a European solution. The Americans were generous after the war, creating the Marshall plan to help the rebuilding of war-torn Europe. This should be the basis of Europe's response to the immigrant inflow. We need a collective agreement to police the frontiers of the European Union coupled with a more effective aid programme already contemplated to help develop the wealth-creating conditions that could incentivise potential immigrants to stay where they are. A generous programme of this sort could be negotiated to include agreement such as that with Albania to repatriate those who still cross these frontiers. It will not be without controversy. There is a difficult choice between the immediate pressure to alleviate hunger, disease and poverty so evident on the one hand and the longer-term challenges to create employment and wealth stimulating conditions on the other hand, that could persuade the potential immigrants to stay. Those who leave have to pay the smugglers substantial sums. Are there ways whereby our aid programmes could offer to add to these sums to encourage job creating investment in their own country?

The role of the state in the economy

It is easy to see why regulation is so prized as a weapon in the hands of populists. Bureaucrats are easy meat, particularly to the small business community wrestling often late at night with the complexity of forms. Turn them into foreign bureaucrats and every nationalist blood cell is stirred to life. If you can mix it all up with immigrants you have that melting pot that throughout history has been responsible for the worst excesses of savagery and bitterness.

The truth is that regulation is what separates civilised society from the law of the jungle. Rules and standards are detailed and complex because civil servants know that there is an army of lawyers out there searching for loopholes and a tiny number of citizens anxious to exploit them. Every minister knows that if those loopholes are exploited successfully it is they who will be called to account.

The report into the Grenfell Tower tragedy will soon be published. This will provide the clearest opportunity to understand the meaning of and responsibility for our regulatory climate. It will throw into sharp relief all those facile claims about so-called light touch regulation when the demand for tighter rules and closer implementation lead the headlines. Recently the security of the banking system and the quality of our rivers and waterways have focused attention on the need of tighter not lighter regulation.

It is little wonder that against this background of unfolding events public opinion has changed significantly. There are difficult balances to be struck between competing goals. In the present state of the British economy, it is important to recognise the role of public expenditure in the quest for the economic growth upon which living standards depend. I write from the perspective of a minister who served in three Conservative governments.

A common experience in my jobs made me confront the

challenges facing the dramatic rate of technological change that will affect every aspect of our life. Artificial intelligence, cryptocurrencies, cyber-crime, gene editing are part of a world beyond my experience. But, whenever I have had to face the consequences of research and development, I have been forced to recognise the sometimes pivotal importance of public expenditure. Governments, universities and the private sector all play essential roles but the thrust into much of the future is financed by governments and their agencies. Britain is now among the leaders of a group of medium-sized economies dwarfed by the United States and China.

As Minister of Aerospace I saw Rolls–Royce go bust in the 1970s because it decided its commercial future depended on its ability to compete with Boeing's CF6 engine. That engine was developed for and by the American defence budget. Rolls–Royce borrowed the money as a commercial endeavour to produce the RB211. It proved too much. Ted Heath was right to save the company, which he saw as a strategic asset and which today remains the beating heart of what is best about British engineering.

As minister responsible for space at that time I was asked to finance a British project. I asked how much Europe spent on space in total compared with the United States. The combined budget of the European nations was $200 million. The United States was spending six times as much. I persuaded our European partners to share our resources and create the European Space Agency. This country secured the lead in satellite development.

As Secretary of State for Defence I was involved in the development of President Reagan's Star Wars project. This was a proposal to intercept and destroy incoming missiles threatening America and its allies. I have no criticism of a country that seeks to defend its airspace. General Abrahamson explained that he had almost $30 billion to assemble the necessary facilities and expertise for the task. He offered to place a £100 million contract with Herriot–Watt University in Edinburgh to partner the United States in one technologically advanced programme where the Scots were at the world's cutting edge.

He did not say it but I realised that he knew where such excellence existed everywhere in the world and he would seek to create similar partnerships wherever he could. The consequence would be an extraordinary inflow of technological excellence into American industry. It is a familiar theme of the Brexit case that we should be free to create a Silicon Valley on the Thames. Brexit has already cut us off from European research programmes and that is before one asks where the public expenditure is coming from by way of compensation. The original Silicon Valley was underpinned by the American Defence and Space programmes.

Of course, the energy and ingenuity of the American private sector has brilliantly exploited this incredible underpinning but it was public funding that created Silicon Valley and the former that thrived on it. The controversy that has arisen over President Biden's massive subsidy to American industry to finance the next generation of non-polluting cars is a rerun of this phenomenon. The European Union will do the same. The simple truth is that we cannot afford to initiate and develop the advancing technological programmes that will change our lifestyles and create countless jobs in the future on our own. Our self-interest is best served by participation in collaborative projects with countries with similar self-interests.

Devolving power

The United Kingdom has its own domestic agenda. It is now widely recognised that our over-centralised concentration of power in London is no longer acceptable. My experience of local government began in 1968 with the publication of the

Redcliffe-Maud report into the structure of local government in England. This examined a structure evolved throughout history to reflect the conditions of the time. Well into the second half of the twentieth century the report examined an administrative structure dating back to a time when the only means of transportation was by foot or horse. Change had created the counties in the Local Government Act of 1888 but the historic infrastructure of some 1,300 authorities remained. Redcliffe-Maud recommended that they should be replaced by sixty unitary authorities. The incoming Conservative government in 1970 chose a substantial but less radical solution, which created two-tier counties and districts with conurbation wide authorities in the metropolitan areas involving some 300 authorities. As a junior minister I supported Peter Walker in executing this reform. Seven years later, by then Secretary of State myself, I got rid of these metropolitan authorities in the search for simplicity and the elimination of bureaucracy. I now regard that as a mistake and I have spent the rest of my political career helping to recreate such authorities administered by directly elected mayors.

Tony Blair's Labour government in 2000 created just such a Mayoralty in London and David Cameron later moved the agenda seriously forward. George Osborne and Greg Clark placed the devolution agenda high on their list of priorities, not only negotiating new mayoral authorities in metropolitan areas but by incentivizing the process by the introduction of longer-term funding unrelated to specific functions.

In his budget in March 2023, Jeremy Hunt described the state of devolution with the following words. 'I will also boost mayors' financial autonomy by agreeing multi-year single settlements for the West Midlands and the Greater Manchester Combined Authority in the next spending review, something I intend to roll out for all mayoral areas over time.' I have waited a long time to hear those words. I hope the Labour Party will endorse them.

Looking back, it is easy to recognise the critical experience that changed my perspective. Like most ministers my first experience started from a vantage point in a specialist functional department, in my case the Ministry of Transport. The Ministry had close links locally through the County Surveyors and there was a full and exciting policy agenda awaiting attention. My colleagues in other ministries each had their own specific link to local administration. Home Office to Chief Constable, Treasury to Director of Finance, Department of Education to Director of Education and so on. The system seemed to work, although no other capitalist economy took so functional approach to the relationship between central and local government.

The riots of 1981 shook the body politic. The police had to be supported in the restoration of law and order but I persuaded Mrs Thatcher that I should take a closer look. I walked the streets of Liverpool, scene of some of the worst disturbances. Everyone knew what was wrong but it was always down to someone else. I drew some clear conclusions. First, there was no one effectively in charge. Second, there was no machinery at either national or local level to co-ordinate what could serve as a local strategy built on the very different local circumstances. Third, significant parts of the local community including the private sector, the universities and the quangos played little part in creating or influencing the community of which they were a part.

In a series of reports to government I have set out detailed recommendations to improve this. A common, but controversial, factor was the introduction of directly elected mayors, common practice in similar economies overseas. I believe it important to ensure such a local leader has to appeal across the local electorate, to be recognised as responsible and judged by results. The present party-political divide can lead to a position where, assured of a majority of council seats, it is possible for the party in power to take little interest in areas represented by their political opponents. This does not serve to unify and stimulate a community culture.

The question remains how to improve the governance of this country. Brexiteers said that Europe would disintegrate into its original nations. The Euro was once seen as the harbinger of the EU's breakup. Actually, far from disintegration, countries are queuing to join. The savagery that followed the breakup of Yugoslavia towards the end of the last century and the current tragedy of Ukraine are the clearest examples of the triumph of the unity of Europe. Somewhere over the rainbow we need to find an accord with Russia.

The question today is not whether a united Europe can survive but whether the United Kingdom can. Sinn Fein is now the largest party in the Northern Ireland Assembly. The Scottish Nationalists use identical arguments that underlie the Brexit case to break up the United Kingdom. The threat may well have been diminished by the departure of Nicola Sturgeon but that is not certain.

I have no experience of devolution as it has worked in practice in Scotland, Wales and Northern Ireland. My impression, however, is that devolution has in practice merely moved the London top-down model to the devolved authorities. For London, insert Edinburgh, Cardiff or Belfast. Without being definitive about precise maps it seems to me that in Scotland real effective devolution would lead to partnerships between Edinburgh on the one hand and Edinburgh, Glasgow, Dundee, Aberdeen and the Highlands on the other, while Wales would see partnerships between Cardiff as the capital city with Cardiff, Swansea, Mid-Wales, North Wales and Pembrokeshire on the other.

Conclusion

I do not accept that Brexit is irreversible. The timescale may be unpredictable. Controversy is certain. We have seen recently an indication of what is to come. A group of senior politicians from across the parties and Brexit divide met with senior business people at what purported to be a secret conference at Ditchley Park. Of course, it was no such thing, as anyone who has attended one of their conferences can attest. It gave the Brexiteers the excuse for howls of mock rage. *The Daily Telegraph* was predictably indignant, although the force of its wrath was counterbalanced by a leading article by Sherelle Jacobs, headlined 'Brexit is dead.' Inside the paper, in another article, was a quote from Jonathan Haskel, a member of the Bank of England's Monetary Policy Committee, claiming that Brexit had cost the average family £1,000. *The Daily Mail* was as outraged as *The Telegraph* but only headlined the Labour Party attendees leaving the presence of senior Tories to the small print. Hints here of the coming election campaign!

It will take time to repair the economic and reputational damage of Brexit but our purpose must be clear. We are and always have been a European power. We must reclaim our position at the centre of Europe. We must start by rebuilding bridges. Rishi Sunak has shown how courtesy and civilised behaviour can change the basis of our relationship. I am encouraged by the practical compromise reached over the Irish border. I hope it will lead to the restoration of a devolved government and enable the Northern Ireland economy to recover against a background of stability.

The President of the European Commission has said that this agreement will now open the way to end the isolation of our scientists and researchers, with the UK rejoining the Horizon Europe research and innovation programmes, including the European Research Council strand, which pre-Brexit had been providing key opportunities to our brightest and best and attracting their counterparts from Europe and beyond to UK universities. This is very welcome. But we should also restore the right of our young people to participate in projects abroad under the EU's Erasmus Plus programme.

In place of a Department for Exiting the EU we need a minister with responsibility for enhancing relationships with the EU. That rescue operation could start with a veterinary agreement to reduce checks on food products entering the single market. That would help farmers and food producers across the UK, including providing a further boost to Northern Ireland. It could also explore a more generous visa system to help with the chronic shortage of skilled people throughout the public and private sectors – the NHS in particular. We should seek to remove the restrictions on musicians and other UK service providers and performers to work for short periods in the EU. Each of the steps I have set out is realistic and draws our self-interests closer.

The EU is still there, next door, with its market of 450 million people. We thrive together by working together. The world faces challenges of unprecedented scale. No nation state of our size and resource can meet these alone. But the opportunities of an ever more sophisticated, technologically empowered, peaceful future are also on offer. We owe it to future generations to ensure they play the fullest part in that inheritance. That demands playing a European part.

People say to me that they are thinking of going into politics. I advise against. Just thinking about it does not display the certainty and determination to enjoy and succeed in a world of relentless pressure and continuing controversy. Most of the decisions that ministers take are those that no one else can. By their nature they demand the resolution of issues where people have deeply held views and where substantial resources are at stake. Those who agree with your decision are grateful and polite. Those who disagree will not forget. After the experience of six decades in the frontline I wish I could live it all again. There are huge challenges. There always were and there always will be. It is a privilege beyond measure to have been able to help nudge history just a little in the direction I wanted it to go.

10

What Divides the Centre Right from the Centre Left (and what doesn't)

Daniel Finkelstein

The debate on assisted dying had been going on in the House of Lords for many hours when the Justice Minister Lord Wolfson of Tredegar rose to reply. He came quickly to the point.

What the Lords had been hearing were suggestions that a new law would threaten the lives of older people. They might be pressured into ending their life earlier than they really wished to. But the Lords had also been hearing of the consequences of forbidding assisted dying. Many peers told stories of relatives who had suffered at the end of their life because they weren't allowed medical assistance to end it.

So, said Wolfson, this was how it stood: 'I hope we are united in wanting to protect the rights of vulnerable people from direct or indirect pressure to commit suicide. The central issue, therefore, is whether a blanket ban on assisting suicide is a necessary and proportionate way of achieving this.' It was a brilliant way of summarizing the entire debate. But it was more than that. It was a brilliant argument for the political centre.

What Lord Wolfson was pointing out is that the policy of assisted dying has risks as well as advantages, so the choice involves balancing the two against each other. You can reduce the risks to a great extent, but not eliminate them entirely. And that leaves the task of weighing the risk that remains against the clear advantages. And what is true of assisted dying is true of almost every policy dispute.

The core politics of the centre

A good example came shortly after the election of the Coalition government in 2010. The Chancellor, George Osborne, proposed that higher-rate taxpayers no longer receive child benefit (the policy was somewhat more complicated than that, but that was the essence). This seemed a useful way of reducing public spending, with the burden of the reduction falling mainly on the better off. But there was a problem.

A two-earner household might have greater income than a single-earner one. Yet if both of the two earners have individual incomes below the higher rate threshold, they might retain child benefit, whatever their total household income. Meanwhile, the single-earner, if they were above the threshold, would lose the benefit. This didn't seem fair. Again, there were ways of mitigating this problem but not of eliminating it altogether. So, it came down to a choice – to go ahead with the policy on the grounds that the advantages outweighed the problems, or not to go ahead with it.

Most policy decisions, in other words, come down to a judgement about mitigation and proportionality. There are tensions in everything. There are few controversies – perhaps restricted to disputes about matters of fact – in which only one side has any merit at all. It is understanding this, and living with its implications, that is the core of the politics of the centre.

First it leads to support for a liberal democratic constitution that allows different arguments, opinions and interests to find expression and representation. This should be based on the rule of law, safeguarded by independent institutions and resisting the arbitrary power of factions or autocrats. This is stressed both by David Gauke in his introduction and by Dominic Grieve in his chapter.

Second, it supports freedom of ideas and exchange, which can only be sustained by a market economy that allows competition and choice. This should be international, because creativity and ideas do not stop at borders. Andrew Cooper goes as far as to argue in this book that the future of politics is a debate between those who believe in openness and those who resist it.

Third, it stands in opposition to populism of left and right. Populism argues that there is a single simple and identifiable will of the people (albeit they differ about what it is), while centrists insist upon the importance of pluralism and grappling with complexity. The importance of the distinction between populism and the centre is why Rory Stewart devoted of all of his chapter to the subject.

Fourthly, it relies on the ability to make competent judgements based on available evidence. It favours also the pursuit of knowledge and respect for facts.

Compromise and Complexity

Finally, it insists on the value of mitigation and compromise. Centrists are often accused of being buffeted about by the extremes, with the content of centrism being determined by contending extremes. This is not entirely true, as I've already argued. Centrism leads to belief in a liberal democratic market economy. But there is an element of truth in it. Centrists argue unashamedly that there is a benefit to getting contending interests to compromise with each other. And, this will sometimes involve adopting a middle course between two or more alternatives. Or reaching a compromise when others are clashing.

Balancing the advantages and mitigating the disadvantages of different courses – because centrists are inclined to acknowledge that opposing courses of action may both have advantages – has great merit. It may get closer to a workable solution that makes the most of all the possibilities, and softens any problems. And – not to be overlooked – it may make more people feel they can live with the outcome.

A stable society that respects the rule of law relies on people being willing, at the very least, to abide by laws even when they don't agree. It's reasonable to have some regard to this. And so centrists should not be embarrassed to favour compromise. This could be a much better position than being swept along by one side or the other. The correct centrist response to the famous accusation that people who stand in the middle of the road get run over is – 'not if it is a dual carriageway'. Centrists adhere to this position because of its merits, but it is an additional advantage that it is also electorally strong. Competence and compromise, in particular, have broad appeal. Arguing that a political party ought to move to the centre is, therefore, usually arguing that it act in its own best interests. But this is not the primary advantage of the centrist position. The primary advantage is that the centrist position does best at dealing with complexity. And this will not always appeal, or appeal to everyone. We are going through a moment, right now, when the politics of the centre is being challenged particularly strongly.

In her book, *Twilight of Democracy*, Anne Applebaum identifies trouble at dealing with complexity as one of the main reasons why people turn towards extremism and authoritarianism. Isaiah Berlin, she says, 'observed that not all of the things that human beings think are good or desirable are compatible. Efficiency, liberty, justice, equality, the demands of the individual, and the demands of the group – all these things push us in different directions.' Applebaum goes on to quote Berlin himself on why this is difficult for some people to accept. 'To admit that the fulfilment of some of our ideals may in principle make the fulfilment of others impossible is to say that the notion of total human fulfilment is a formal contradiction, a metaphysical chimera.' To this Applebaum adds: 'Nevertheless, unity is a chimera that some will always pursue.'

Different kinds of centrists

Yet, accepting the truth of Berlin's observation, as centrists do, is only the beginning. Wolfson's example, calling for a judgement on the proportionality of a blanket ban on assisted dying, illustrates why. The judgement is subjective.

There will, of course, first be a debate about the evidence and the efficacy of any proposed mitigation of the effects of an assisted dying law. Some will argue that the law has been instituted elsewhere and the mitigation hasn't worked. Others will view the same evidence and suggest it has. People's interpretation of the evidence will be influenced by what they wish to believe, but in principle consideration of the evidence is capable of objective judgement and resolution.

Not so the choice of the balance to be struck in creating the policy. There will be some who regard as unacceptable even quite small amounts of risk that someone might be pressured to die early. While others (as it happens, my position) might view the ban on assisted dying as imposing so much suffering that small amounts of risk are worth incurring. The centrist accepts that there is no single correct balance to be struck. Different people, based on their own experience, or their upbringing or their social background, will have different views of what is proportionate. There is no objective solution, no final answer.

The centre right and the centre left share the view that many (in fact almost all) political issues are like this. They share suspicion of extremists and absolutists who reject this complexity.

But on big issues they differ in the emphasis they put and the judgements they make. In other words, the centre left and centre right believe in the Wolfson test of proportionality, but differ over what is proportionate.

Before looking at just a few of these issues and the way that right and left diverge, it is worth considering a different question – do right and left really exist at all? There are really two objections to the idea of left and right. The first is that the terms seem to treat politics as linear, with voters and positions laid out in a long line. It is odd to advance the idea of complexity and then adopt such a simple notion. Clearly political positions exist in multiple dimensions.

The second, and related objection, is that to suggest there are centre right positions on, say, tax rates and nuclear defence, assumes that people's views on these issues are correlated. And there is a good deal of evidence to show that they aren't. Voters are not particularly ideological. They may not have a position on tax rates at all, certainly not a consistent one. And there is no policy reason that if they did, it would be related to their view on defence. Indeed, favouring low taxes and a lot of defence spending are positions that pull in different directions. The evidence of this in political science is strong (it is captured quite well, for instance, by Christopher Achen and Larry Bartels) and, again, it wouldn't be very centrist to ignore evidence.

But, as long as the terms centre right and centre left aren't taken too literally as meaning there is a spectrum of views, and as long as the claim of consistency isn't too great, then I think the terms are just about descriptive enough to be useful. I think for whatever reason – people in particular groups copying each other, say, or forming coalitions – the terms do have meaning, at least among politically engaged people. And the strongest piece of evidence for that is that people use the terms to describe others, and when they do, the descriptions help. They intuitively make sense and seem quite good descriptions of real people and ideas. And, for this reason, the terms have endured despite the strength of the objections to them.

Centre right and centre left

What, then, are some of the big differences between centre right and centre left and why do I, overall at least, incline to the former over the latter? Here are a few examples. The best place to start is with the question of the size and scope of government.

Centrists share some views about the economy – there isn't much alternative to an exchange economy based on property rights; ensuring private enterprise has an incentive to succeed produces greater overall prosperity; a market economy is dependent on an infrastructure much of which needs to be commonly funded; there is a minimum level of income below which no one should fall; gross inequalities make a healthy democracy difficult and need to be remedied; and there are basic public services to which access should be guaranteed. Yet these produce obvious tensions. Reducing gross inequalities may also reduce incentives to succeed. Public services are essential and right but it is possible to spend all of national income on public services. At which point nobody will bother making any money.

The need to ensure a minimum household income provides possibly the best example. The point at which people are comfortable with their minimum guaranteed state income may also be the point at which a large number of people stop working. The Wolfson question arises – is a low level or even no level of minimum income a proportionate response to the risk of people stopping work? You can mitigate the risk in some ways – governments are constantly announcing new work tests for benefit recipients – but you cannot eliminate it.

A similar example is provided by the debate over the appropriate tax burden to place on top earners. The provision of well-financed public services is to a large extent dependent upon the contribution made by those with the greatest means. But at a certain point high marginal tax rates becomes a disincentive to earning. Some of the judgements about the appropriate tax rates are empirical ones – what really is the impact of high tax rates on effort and creativity? But others are about the taste for security and risk.

All centrists acknowledge that there are unresolvable tensions in determining the extent of government spending and intervention. There is never, in practice, a point at which an extra pound of public spending wouldn't procure something of value. But there is also never a point at which an extra pound of taxation isn't felt by those who pay it, with an impact on incentives and the ability of taxpayers to choose what they spend money on. There is no single correct solution to the problem. And public opinion shifts, making even the political choice difficult. But in the end, decisions have to be made.

The centre right and centre left have a lot in common, but they don't always make the same decision. The centre right tends to be more wary of public spending. It isn't opposed to it, or remotely libertarian. Tim Pitt provides an excellent overview of centre right economic thinking in his chapter and Anne Milton grapples with the complexity of health policy in hers. But, at the margin, it is more concerned than is the centre left that public spending will squeeze out enterprise and effort, unless government takes a firm approach to all the many demands on it that are made.

The same thinking governs attitudes towards regulation. All centrists accept the need for regulation, but those on the centre right are more concerned about the effect it might have on creativity and even on voluntary good deeds. The centre left accuses the right of being insufficiently concerned about the common good, a charge the right rejects as unfair. We simply believe that not every demand can be acceded to. A robust approach is necessary to ensure that spending and regulation don't become out of control. What the centre left sees as complacency and even heartlessness, the centre right views as sensible restraint. This debate becomes particularly fierce when the centre right holds office at times of fiscal crisis and wishes to ensure the state is solvent. This can lead it to support both tax rises and spending cuts.

The centre left shares the view that some sort of balance is needed, and agrees that neither spending increases or tax cuts will magically pay for themselves. But it is generally more optimistic that any borrowing can be quickly brought under control. It often accuses the centre right of being unduly harsh, even relishing the word 'no' for ideological reasons. The centre right finds this criticism irritating, responding that saying 'yes' to too many demands is dishonest and short termist.

This difference is as much one of temperament as of ideology. The centre right has the same generosity of spirit and compassion that motivates the centre left, but is more cautious, we would say more realistic. It is more concerned about the negative impacts of any action it might take and less optimistic about the results of acting on good intentions. This difference can also be found in the debate about constitutional reform.

With its somewhat greater restlessness and concern about the status quo, and its greater confidence in the ability of humans to create rational systems that bring mankind's arrangements closer to perfection, the centre left is attracted to constitutional reform.

Indeed, because the centre left is often fighting off attacks from within the left that it is too conservative on spending and tax, it finds constitutional reform particularly tempting. It offers the ability to match radical rhetoric about change and hope, while resisting fiscally imprudent schemes. The centre right accepts the need to update constitutional arrangements as social tastes and economic relationships change. But it is much more naturally cautious about its impact, and much less carried away by rhetoric about radical change.

Centrists all want a liberal democratic settlement that protects individual freedom, and reflects public opinion. The centre right is more impressed by the untidy but workable settlement we have, while the centre left is more dissatisfied and more willing to experiment. The centre left accuses the centre right of complacency and defending its own interests. The centre right responds that the centre left is too impressed by paper schemes and not impressed enough by the stability existing arrangements secure.

The so-called culture wars touch on some of the same issues. Centrists acknowledge that British history contains moments that it can be very proud of and moments where its leadership acted shamefully. In other words that our history is complicated. And there are natural tensions between acknowledging the country's errors and taking pride in its past. No centrist takes a simple or faddish view and all find it irritating and even sometimes offensive when people either insist that the country is irredeemably bad, or that it is mere perfection. All can see the value in a more nuanced approach. There is, however, a discernible difference between centre right and centre left approaches. These are rooted in different ideas of progress. The left has more interest in radical schemes and more attachment to dreamers, the right is inclined to reject such schemes and to be sceptical about dreams.

As a result the centre right views the mistakes of the past as contributing to the success of the future. Institutions evolve. The country's entire history, good and bad, makes a contribution to a better today and an even better tomorrow. It is not mere sentiment, therefore, that leads the centre right to be reluctant (although by no means always flatly opposed) to concede too much ground to those who wish to pull down statues or rename buildings.

A degree of scepticism and caution about the negative consequences of new arrangements also informs the centre right's approach to social liberalism. Centrists are generally pragmatic, reject fundamentalism, respect the diversity of individuals and the common humanity of very different people. We believe strongly in pluralism and are well disposed to those seeking civic equality and personal freedom. The centre right and centre left are often closely aligned on such issues, but on the right there is more hesitation before agreeing to change. There is more concern to ensure that changes in social attitudes are solid and durable before the state adapts to them.

The centre right, not entirely to its credit, can be slow to accept social change, but, certainly to its credit, then embraces it fully. It was the centre right that introduced equal votes for women, for example, and gay marriage.

A rather similar difference can be found in the approach to international institutions. Across the centre there is a common understanding of the value of international co-operation and some pooling of sovereignty (as reflected in Michael Heseltine's chapter), combined with a realisation that there is a tension between that and both national identity and decentralised power. But there are differences. The centre right is somewhat more cautious in agreeing to transfers of sovereignty to international bodies. And there is a particular concern, not held by the centre left to the same degree, that while on paper global institutions might be accountable, in practice they are out of the reach of most people who don't have the social capital or mindset to allow them to judge or influence the politics of continents. Conservative temperament makes the centre right prefer tried and tested national institutions to vague internationalist rhetoric.

There are many other areas – environmental policy (as in Amber Rudd's chapter), international diplomacy, defence – where this same difference can be found. All centrists recognise the tensions between action and inaction, between progressive aspiration and realism, between the advantages of optimism and those of pessimism, with the centre right somewhat more sceptical about the perfectibility of mankind and of mankind's arrangements. As a result the conclusions of the centre right and centre left are often quite similar, or even actually the same. No one should be in the slightest bit embarrassed by that. Nor that we are engaged in a debate across the centre where we understand each other and can differ in a civilised way. There probably should be more ways for people to communicate with each other across the centre.

Political divisions

However, a big constraint upon this communication across the centre results from perhaps the biggest difference between the centre right and the centre left – the choice of coalition partners. Partly because of the electoral system, British politics tends to divide between right and left with the centre right allying with other people on the right rather than with other people in the centre. This means that the most vigorous debate has been, say, on the differences between the centre right and centre left on public spending. And less vigorous on those things that divide the centre from populists on left and right. This is quite natural and may persist, but it is increasingly obvious that there are many things that unite the centre and require a common defence: the importance of the rule of law, the protection of individual rights, the openness of our trading system, the centrality of science, the importance of facts. All these things are under heavy populist attack.

The centre right and centre left have to find ways of mounting this defence, and helping each other to do so, even inside the current party system. We should be less embarrassed by making common cause across parties, building networks and sharing ideas. A firm rejection of those who seek to undermine civic norms – those who do not value integrity in public life, who make free speech more difficult, who engage in demagogy rather than reasoned debate – should be part of this common cause. The centre has a common interest in anything which defends a plural democracy and rejects the simple idea that there is a single will of the people. But the relationship need not only be a negative one, defined by what we both reject.

Conclusion

In the 1970s, New York City went to the brink of bankruptcy. It was dirty, dangerous and declining. Its politics were dominated by competing interest groups, racial division and a vigilante backlash. And then the city was rescued. The cavalry didn't arrive from one flank. It came from centre right and centre left. On the centre left, there were the New Democrats and Bill Clinton determined to reject left extremism, to reform the welfare system and to challenge the grip of the teachers' union on the school system. On the centre right there were Republicans who were more than simple libertarians, and who saw public authorities as having duties that needed to be properly resourced and vigorously conducted.

The result was a suite of policies – broken windows policing and order policy, better street cleaning, incentives to get welfare recipients back to work, school choice – all of which together did much to combat New York's malaise. These policies recognised tensions and complexity, avoided traditional ideological positions, did their best to avoid getting stuck because of petty differences, and as a result made significant progress.

So, a dialogue across the centre and creative co-operation with the centre left is certainly valuable and important. The more urgent task will be a defence of the centre right within the right. And this is not a task that should be abandoned because, just at the moment, it seems hard. Centre right positions – the caution and restraint, the natural conservatism that characterises them – seem to me more valuable now than they have ever been. The centre left's progressivism shows insufficient regard for the advantages of existing institutions, is insufficiently robust in resisting special interests and calls for greater state action and more spending, and is too attracted by paper schemes. There can be allies on the centre left. But no question about what it is that makes us different. Nor any question either of what makes the centre right necessary. And its health and vigour essential to maintain. The case for the centre right remains strong.

Notes

Introduction

1 https://journals.sagepub.com/doi/10.1177/20419058211045127
2 https://ukandeu.ac.uk/wp-content/uploads/2020/06/Mind-the
   -values-gap.pdf

1 The Realignment of British Politics

1 'New class divides in British politics', BES, October 2019. The
   British Election Study is an academic project analysing in detail
   the results of every UK general election since 1964, based on very
   large sample surveys.
2 Tony Blair speech to the TUC Conference, 12 September
   2006.
3 Populus 'Clockface model' demographic analysis.
4 Moisés Naim, *The Revenge of Power*, 2022.
5 Yuval Levin, *The Fractured Republic*, 2017.
6 Margaret Thatcher, Speech to the Conservative Group for
   Europe, 16 April 1975.
7 Dominic Cummings, 'How the Brexit referendum was won',
   Spectator, 9 January 2017.
8 Boris Johnson, 'I cannot stress too much that Britain is part of
   Europe – and always will be', *Daily Telegraph*, 26 June 2016.

9 Margaret Thatcher, Speech to the Conservative Group for Europe, 16 April 1975.

10 British Election Study 1974–75–79 panel study.

11 Dominic Sandbrook, *Seasons in the Sun: The Battle for Britain 1974–1979*, ch. 14, 'The Great Referendum Sideshow', 2012.

12 Margaret Thatcher, Speech to the College of Europe, September 1988.

13 Lord Ashcroft Polls, post-vote 12,000 sample national poll, 24 June 2016.

14 Moisés Naim, *The Revenge of Power*, 2022.

15 Tony Blair, 'Change or decline', speech to Chatham House, January 2021.

16 YouGov poll, 6 April 2023.

17 Matthew Parris, 'The Tories should turn their backs on Clacton', *The Times*, September 2014.

18 Thomas L. Friedman, 'The United Kingdom has gone mad', *New York Times*, April 2019.

3 Restoring the Rule of Law

1 Speech to Inter-Parliamentary Union 18/10/79.

2 Chahal vs. UK 23, EHRR 413.

3 Conservative Party paper, October 2014.

4 Lord Mance, Sir Thomas More Lecture, 2022.

5 UK in a Changing Europe, https://ukandeu.ac.uk/explainers/com pliance-with-the-european-convention-on-human-rights/

6 R vs. Sec of State for Exiting the EU, UKSC5.

7 R vs. the Prime Minister, UKSC41.

4 Fixing a Bad Brexit Deal

1 'Brexit, "Britain was wrong to leave the EU." Agree or disagree?' January 2023. *UnHerd Britain* 2023.

2 Tony Blair Institute: Moving On, Brexit Polling. 18 October 2022. JL Partners.

5 A Renewed Agenda for Conservative Economics

1 Margaret Thatcher, quoted in Conor Burns, 'Margaret Thatcher's greatest achievement: New Labour', *ConservativeHome*, 11 April 2008.

2 Liz Truss, quoted in 'Rishi Sunak attacks Liz Truss's economic credibility', *The National News*, 24 August 2022.

3 Arthur Balfour, Unpublished drafts of a manuscript on political economy, 1907–11?, Balfour papers, Add. MSS49950, fos.10–14.

4 Edmund Burke, *Reflections on the Revolution in France*, 1986, p. 106.

5 Benjamin Disraeli, *Sybil*, 1846.

6 Nigel Lawson, 'The economic perils of thinking for the moment', September 1978.

7 Margaret Thatcher, Speech to the Bow Group, London, May 1978.

8 E.H.H. Green, *Ideologies of Conservatism: Conservative Political Ideas in the Twentieth Century*, 2002, e-book version, ch. 8.

9 'Britain's economic record since 2007 ranks near the bottom among peer countries', *Economist*, 15 December 2022.

10 Torsten Bell et al., 'Help today, squeeze tomorrow', Resolution Foundation, November 2022, p. 5.

11 Juliana Oliveira-Cunha, Jesse Kozler, Pablo Shah, Gregory Thwaites and Anna Valero, *Business Time: How Ready Are UK Firms for the Decisive Decade?*, Resolution Foundation, Economy 2030 Inquiry, November 2021, p. 12.

12 John van Reenen, 'The economic legacy of Margaret Thatcher is a mixed bag', LSE Blog, April 2013.

13 Robert Colville, *The Sunday Times*, 27 March 2022.

14 Tim Pitt, 'The Road to Credibility', *Onward*, November 2022, p. 14.

15 For a discussion of these two structural drivers, see Dietrich Vollrath, *Fully Grown*, 2020.

16 See Erik Brynjolfsson and Andrew McAfee, *The Second Machine Age*, 2014.

17 Robert Gordon, *The Rise and Fall of American Growth*, 2016.

18 ONS, *Household Income Inequality, UK: Financial Year Ending 2021*, 28 March 2022; *World Inequality Database*.

19 OECD, Income Inequality Data.

20 Neil O'Brien, 'Measuring up for levelling up', *Onward*, September 2020, p. 4.

21 ONS, *Household Total Wealth in Great Britain: April 2018 to March 2020*, 7 January 2022.

22 Kwasi Kwarteng, 'The Growth Plan 2022 speech', HM Treasury, 23 September 2022.

23 Research by the OECD has found that intergenerational earnings mobility is lower in countries with higher levels of income inequality. See OECD, 'Divided we stand: Why inequality keeps rising, 2011'; for a discussion of the link between inequality and economic growth, see Era Dabla-Norris, Kalpana Kochhar, Nujin Suphaphiphat, Frantisek Ricka and Evridiki Tsounta, 'Causes and consequences of income inequality: A global perspective', IMF, June 2015

24 Office for Budget Responsibility, 'Economic and fiscal forecast', November 2022, p. 46.

25 OBR, Fiscal risks and sustainability, July 2022, Table 4.7, p. 144 and Table 4.9, p. 147; and Table 4.7 p. 144.

26 OBR, Fiscal risks and sustainability, July 2022, p. 5.

27 OBR, Fiscal risks and sustainability, July 2022, p. 16. This excludes the consolidation announced by Jeremy Hunt in the 2022 Autumn Statement.

28 HM Treasury, *Autumn Budget and Spending Review 2021*, October 2021, p. 39.

29 Competition and Markets Authority, *The State of UK Competition*, April 2022.

30 OECD, *Global Revenue Statistics Database*.

31 Office for Tax Simplification, Inheritance Tax Review – first report, November 2018, p. 5.

32 Mike Brewer, Karl Handscomb, Gavin Kelly, James Smith and Lalitha Try, 'Social insecurity assessing trends in social security

to prepare for the decade of change ahead', January 2022, p. 6 and p. 17.

6 Tackling the Health Crisis

1 ONS, *Health state life expectancies by national deprivation deciles, England: 2018 to 2020.*

2 https://commonslibrary.parliament.uk/research-briefings/sn033 36

3 M. Marmot, J. Allen, T. Boyce, P. Goldblatt and J. Morrison, 'Health equity in England: The Marmot Review 10 years on', Institute of Health Equity, 2020. health.org.uk/publications/reports/the-marmot-review-10-years-on

4 Calendar year 2019 or financial year 2019–2020 are used for many of the figures to illustrate the long-run picture before the covid-related distortions of both expenditure and care.

5 World Bank: https://data.worldbank.org/indicator/SH.XPD.CH EX.GD.ZS?end=2019&locations=US-GB-AU-FR-DE-IT-NL-ES& name_desc=false&start=2009

6 IFS: https://ifs.org.uk/taxlab/taxlab-data-item/components-uk-gov ernment-spending-2019-20

7 World Bank: https://data.worldbank.org/indicator/SH.XPD.GH ED.GD.ZS?end=2019&locations=US-GB&start=2015

7 Winning the Global Race for Science and Technology

1 https://data.worldbank.org/indicator/GB.XPD.RSDV.GD.ZS

Index